A Year at
Ballymaloe
Cookery School

Darina Allen

With photographs by
Melanie Eclare, Michelle Garrett
and Timmy Allen

Kyle Cathie Limited

For my father-in-law Ivan Allen who began
it all and encouraged me every step of the way

Ballymaloe Cookery School is run by mega team work, everyone involved with the
school contributes to the overall magic in their own way. My thanks go, as ever, to the
following people:

To Eileen, Elizabeth and Haulie who are responsible for the wonderful appearance
of the gardens and for the abundance of herbs, fruit and vegetables throughout the
seasons.

To Frank, who nurtures the hens, ducks and geese and coaxes them to produce lots of
eggs and little clutches of chickens and goslings.

To Claire, Iris, Peg, Rachel, Rosemary, Sally and Sue who teach the students, test
recipes, encourage, cajole and are cheerful through sunny and stormy weather.

To Rosalie, my right hand woman, who has been with me since the beginning, and to
Adrienne, who arrived soon after her, both of whom have the unenviable task of organis-
ing my life and keeping me on track, aided and abetted by our receptionist Cathriona.

To Mary and Bessie who pamper and spoil me; to Eleanor who composes poetry as she
irons, Ber and her team who get the cottages looking fresh and lovely for each new
group of students or guests and put a little garden posy of flowers in each room.

To Marie and Doreen who keep us sparkling, to the ever-smiling Grainne who does just
about everything with great humour.

To Will and his building team who seem to manage to create everything from follies to
cafés with the minimum of direction and the motto 'no problem'.

To all my family: my parents-in-law, Ivan and Myrtle, ever an inspiration, ever supportive;
my mother Elizabeth O'Connell, who encouraged me every step of the way; my brother
Rory O'Connell, chef at Ballymaloe House who shares his creativity with me; and to my
children, Isaac, Toby, Lydia and Emily who have inherited a wild and crazy mother –
their smiles and hugs make it all worth the effort.

And last but not least, to my dear Tim who has endured my flights of fancy for more than
26 years now.

This book is a celebration of all their efforts.

*Darina Allen and the Publishers of this book would like to thank the Bank of Ireland for
the generous help with the photography contained in this book.*

Contents

A Note on Ingredients

Our gardens produce endless delights for us throughout the year and every season brings its own rewards. I will never forget the year that Timmy ambled in asking, 'Have you looked at your almond tree recently?' I was wild with excitement when I discovered the first soft, furry, green almonds. Now we have a little almond feast every year.

Quite apart from depending on the wealth of food from our gardens, much of our work at the School would be impossible without the support of our local producers. Take the Irish farmhouse cheese makers for instance, who provide a gorgeous array of delicious produce. Most of them are women, with a few exceptions, and they are a charismatic lot – free spirited and passionate about their craft. I feel truly grateful to these artisans who are prepared to spend long hours making and nurturing their cheese to ensure that each develops to its full potential. So try one of the many varieties they produce from cow, goat and ewe's milk – Milleens, Gubbeen, Durrus, Cashel Blue, Baylough, Desmond, Croghan, Orla, Ardsallagh, Knocklara, Kerry, Cooleeney, Coolea, Abbey Blue, Killorglin, Chetwynd, Ardrahan, Lavistown, Ring, Boilie… there are over 80 to choose from.

It is really good to be frightfully fussy about the important basics in your kitchen. Good quality salt, pepper and oil are incredibly important because they are used in most dishes; careless use of poor quality goods will spoil even the most robust meal. Therefore choose these ingredients carefully.

Salt: we use plain dairy salt in our cooking which has no additives that may mar the flavour of your food. On the table, we use Maldon sea salt or hand-panned sea salt from Brittany.

Pepper: use peppercorns and grind them specially for each dish. Ideally have one mill for black and one for white. They vary enormously so hunt around for really aromatic ones.

Oil: virtually everything sold under the title of 'cooking oil' is of poor quality. Buy good quality sunflower, peanut or pure olive oil for frying and extra virgin oil for dressings, pesto and drizzling.

Vinegar: malt vinegar is fine for pickles and chutneys but wine vinegars, especially wood-aged ones, make a great difference to your recipes. Make your own infused vinegars and oils (see page 184) – they are so easy to prepare and infinitely less expensive than the attractively packaged bottles on the specialist food shelves.

Eggs: the quality of eggs makes a phenomenal difference to the flavour of even the most simple dishes. Always use free-range; better still, if you live in the country, get a few hens! They will eat your scraps and reward you with delicious eggs.

Sugar: soft brown Barbados sugar sprinkled over porridge, apple tart or yoghurt magically transforms these staple foods.

Honey: the number of different flavoured honeys you can get is a revelation. The taste is affected by the flowers from which the bees collect their pollen. Our local honey is predominantly apple blossom, heather or mixed flowers from west Cork.

Chocolate: choose brands with a high percentage of cocoa solids – we use Valrhona, Lesmé, Meunier, Suchard and Lindt.

Cream: Irish dairy products are still superb quality. The cream that we get from our local creamery is essentially double cream (about 42% butter fat). Single cream whips softly but double cream is the richest and has the best flavour. Use sparingly. Whipping cream is another alternative.

Butter: we use both salted and unsalted Irish butter; the flavour is wonderful. Seek it out in your shops – it is sold under the 'Kerrygold' label.

The success of the recipes in this book depends upon sourcing really good, naturally produced ingredients so be a fussy shopper and remember that there is no point in buying or growing organically produced food and then boiling the hell out of it!

I have given both metric and imperial measurements, so choose whichever you prefer, but stick to one or the other as they are not interchangeable.

Introduction

Since the beginning at Ballymaloe House and the Cookery School, we have always cooked in harmony with the seasons and sourced as much of the food as possible from our own gardens, farm and greenhouses. It seemed the most natural and logical thing to do. And what we don't produce ourselves we source locally. Our first 'port of call' is Patrick and Mary Walsh's little farm across the road from the cookery school. They grow wonderful spring rhubarb, summer berries and floury potatoes – British Queens, Home Guard, Golden Wonders and Kerr's Pinks. We have built up a whole network of artisan producers who rear free-range chicken, ducks, geese and turkeys for us as well as farmhouse cheesemakers and fish smokers. Others produce sausages, salami, chorizo and cured meats. When the artisan producers come to the school to deliver their produce we introduce them to the students, 'this is Nora Aherne who rears these wonderful ducks', so they can put a face to a name. This is all part of the plot to encourage the students to think about how their food is produced and where it comes from.

The 12-week course students (aimed at those who wish to have the option to earn their living from their cooking) are introduced to the gardeners and farm manager on the first morning and then they are taught how to sow vegetable seeds. They watch them grow week by week during the course. I know of no better way to give people a respect for food or those who grow it than to give someone a seed and let them watch it grow. The reality of the impact of the weather, type of soil and the sheer hard work and how long it takes before its ready to harvest, gradually dawns. Unless the soil is rich and fertile you won't have clean water or good food; this is a fundamentally important lesson for all who cook. When you get it into the kitchen, you will be much more careful to treat food with respect.

Over the years I have become much more concerned about the impact of the cheap food policy on the quality of our food. Since the 1950s, farmers have been encouraged to produce the highest yields for the lowest cost, with disastrous results for both flavour and wellbeing. Consequently, much of our food is nutritionally defi-cient and much less complex in terms of flavour. It became blindingly obvious to me that being organic is not a luxury, it is a necessity, not only from the health point of view but also for the 'wow' factor on the plate. If you start off with mass-produced, denatured food then you need to be a magician to make it taste good, that's where all the chef's twiddles and bows and smarties on top come in – to compensate for the lack of flavour in the basic ingredients. If, on the other hand, you start with fresh, naturally produced, local food in season, then it is so easy to make it taste good.

In 1996, having been inspired by a visit to the San Francisco Farmers' Market, I started the first of the new generation of Farmers' Markets in the Coal Quay in Cork, with a small group of people, including my spirited mother-in-law Myrtle Allen. The movement has burgeoned in an extraordinary way – there are now about 120 in Ireland. In 2001 we started another Farmers' Market just 15 miles from the cookery school in Midleton, Co Cork. At weekends I am regularly on 'my stall with my shawl' and now the certificate students have the opportunity to come with me to learn how to set up and trade at a Farmers' Market.

(ABOVE) Sorrel can be used in soups and sauces and as a salad leaf. It has a wonderfully sharp clean taste. There are many varieties at Ballymaloe. We grow three of them, Buckler Leaf Sorrel (Rumex scutatus) , Sheep's Sorrel (Rumex acetosella) and a common, or Broad-leafed Sorrel, (Rumex acetosa). All are delicious, but the most refreshing of all is the Wild Sorrel (Rumex acetosa) which we pick in the apple orchard and along the cliffs at Ballyandreen.

In March 1999 we joined the Irish Organic Trust with the farm becoming fully certified as organic by March 2001. We have extensive vegetable, fruit and herb gardens, orchards, and greenhouses, and it has became a top priority to grow as much of our raw materials as possible. We have beehives in the orchard for honey: our son Toby looks after the bees and shares his knowledge with interested students. Rare breed pigs – Gloucester Old Spot, Red Duroc, Saddleback, and Black Berkshire crosses – roam freely in fields by the greenhouses and enjoy the end of crops and home-grown grain. Several flocks of free-range hens feed on scraps from the cookery school and produce superb eggs and the odd clutch of chicks. More recently, we have been rearing our own poultry for the table with delicious results. We have had cattle on our farm since 1995 but, in 2005, I bought two little Jersey cows to provide milk for the house and cookery school. We sourced an old separator and now have rich Jersey cream to serve with pudding and the remainder is made into wonderful home-made butter. As required by law, we pasteurise the milk for the school but we ourselves drink raw milk, as do our children and grandchildren.

Many of the students come to the school because it is on an organic farm and they value the opportunity not only to cook with fresh home-grown and local produce, but to learn how it is produced. Gradually we have expanded our range of cookery courses during the years. In 2005 we introduced a third 12-week Certificate Course, and now offer one in autumn, spring, and summer. Students come from all four corners of the earth; we've had up to 13 nationalities on a 12-week course, so our little village of Shanagarry becomes very cosmopolitan. The students go out with the gardeners on a rota basis to bring in the herbs, vegetables and fruit for the morning's cooking. Others opt to learn how to milk the cows and make butter and cheese.

In recent years I have noticed a growing interest in learning old skills, so in 2005 we introduced a series of Forgotten Skills courses – How to keep a few chickens in the garden, A Beginner's Guide to Beekeeping, Basic Home Butchery. We have a charismatic German butcher who teaches basic butchery and how to cure a pig in a 1-day courses, in which he works from the nose to the tail, making wet and dry bacon cures, ham and cured hams – eg prosciutto and serrano, salami, chorizo, home-made sausages, country terrine, brawn etc. Our home smoking course has also been a brilliant success and we've had fun showing people how to build a simple smoker and smoke food in everything from biscuit tins to galvanized dustbins. There is a renewed interest in keeping chickens in your garden too. We bought a small incubator and now we hatch out a batch of chicks on every course, much to the delight of the students – the majority of whom have never seen a chick emerge from an egg.

In the gardens and greenhouse we continue to expand our range of vegetables and fruit. On winter evenings we pore over seed catalogues to choose the best varieties. We grow for flavour rather than yield alone. Last year we grew over 40 different heirloom tomatoes, 10 varieties of basil, several varieties of beetroot, zucchini, aubergine and cucumbers, a huge variety of greens: chard, spinach, kale, cabbage, calabrese, sprouting broccolis, romanesco cauliflower, and beans of every shape and form. We grow edible flowers for the salads: nasturtiums, chives, marigolds, Johnny jump ups. Peaches and apricots grow on the south wall of the school dining room overlooking the fruit garden. In spring the fruit trees are under-planted with spring bulbs: tiny daffodils, crocus, Iris reticulata, snowdrops… then the almond tree flowers, followed by the apples, plums and mulberry. Green gooseberries are ready to eat in May when the elderflowers are blossoming in the perimeter hedge. The currants and berries fruit in June and July for compôtes, jams and jellies. In August the greengage and plum trees are laden and then there is the apple harvest. We still have an old orchard from our commercial apple growing days which produces abundant crops of Bramley's Seedling and Worcester Pearmain, but there are also about 30 old varieties behind the wild flower meadow and trained over arches in the fruit garden. Egremont Russet is an abundant cropper even in poor years. Other favourites are Pitmaston Pine Apple, Lane's Prince Albert, Arthur Turner, Irish Peach, Ard Cairn Russet, Cox's Orange Pippin, Lady Sudley and of course the Beauty of Bath. We have also built some raised beds below the café where the keener students can grow some vegetables and herbs during the course.

Throughout the year, but particularly in autumn, we go foraging for wild berries, nuts, greens, mushrooms, seaweeds and sea vegetables. The foraging course and mushroom hunt are a regular feature of every autumn. This year we added how to produce your own ciders and fruit wines and vinegars so we have a demijohn of home-made cider bubbling by the Aga in my kitchen. We also made sloe gin and lots of fruit liqueur and ratafias to add to the jollity of the festive season.

This is all part of re-educating people about the wonder of how good food is produced.

(BELOW) We are lucky enough to have many glorious types of campanulas in several colors – blues, purples, and whites are the most common. Campanulas grow very easily if they like your soil. These Queen Elizabeth roses also make a spectacular show in the summer months.

Spring

Once I've found the first snowdrop under the beech trees down by the pond, I know that Spring is round the corner; we have a particularly early variety given to me by the mother of Hazel, my sister-in-law. There are wonderful double snowdrops which have survived since the Strangmans lived in this house and created the garden in the 1830s, and I bet that they did not consider the snowdrops would still be cheering the wild and crazy woman who has inherited their garden so many years later.

Ballymaloe Cookery School wakes up in the New Year with the first of our two three-month certificate courses, when some 44 keen students arrive full of excitement and fill the cottages in our courtyard, eager to learn, yet a little apprehensive on the first day. We always say a little silent prayer that the weather will be nice that day. One of the first things they do is visit the greenhouses and the vegetable garden – and I see immediately how bereft the garden is of produce. We pick the Cottier's Kale, sometimes known as 'cut-and-come' and 'hungry gap' because it provides

an endless supply of dark green vegetable when there is little else fresh. Our staff of 26 is made up of many ex-students who've married local people, so our contribution has been to bring a bit of new blood into the area!

The approach of spring promises new vegetables and fruits. Fresh green watercress and tender nettles and sorrel appear, and the slightly wary students learn to make delicious, iron-rich soups. I got my terracotta sea kale and rhubarb forcing pots from Whichford Pottery in England, so now we can have supplies in time for the salmon season, shortly after St Patrick's Day. The little chives start pushing through the soil and we add the flowers to our salads, making a glorious dash of rich purple and white. We've lots of lambs lettuce and the deeply serrated oriental green, mysticana, to liven up the early spring salads. I love the clean taste of the February citrus fruits – the pink grapefruits from Texas, the blood oranges from Spain and clementines and mandarines and ugli fruits, so good and versatile when they are in season. Of course we make marmalade and I adore the smell of it cooking. We make our own bread every day, all year round, lovely sourdough breads, yeast breads; I hope it is true to say that none of the students goes away from the School without a thorough knowledge of breadmaking skills and the immense pleasure to be had from baking. Who can forget the wonderful smells that waft from the oven when a loaf is just baked to perfection?

Some of the land around here has never been turned in living memory. It is full of many different kinds of wild grass, wild herbs and flowers that come up in the springtime; quite lovely. Michael Cuddigan, our third or fourth generation traditional butcher from Cloyne, buys cattle raised on these pastures and they have more flavour than the ones raised in fields with just two or three grasses to eat. Mr Cuddigan provides our meat for the School and Ballymaloe House. We make big cassoulets and stews at this time, flavoured with herbs from the garden; one vegetable after another starts to appear and from having so little at the beginning of spring we are suddenly faced with variety – so many good things you simply cannot harvest them fast enough.

Left: Ballymaloe Cookery School is about 1km (800 yards) from the Atlantic Ocean and benefits from the huge wealth of saltwater fish landed at the fishing village, Ballycotton, nearby.

Right: the ten to twelve varieties of chicken provide free-range eggs for the School.

The ducklings hatch! Out come the proud mothers, each with 8 or 10 ducklings in tow. Frank Walsh, who looks after them and all the chickens that roam the gardens, is pleased as Punch. There are many rare breeds of chicken at Ballymaloe Cookery School – they scratch in the yard and lay the vast number of eggs the students use each week. Timmy does the marketing and the provisioning, visiting the marvellous market in Cork City on Wednesdays and coming back laden with goodies. It's a covered market with its labyrinth of lanes behind St Patrick's Street, the workplace for third and fourth generation traders. Along-side them are hippies and the new generation of stallholders. It is possible to buy anything from pigs' tails, skirts and bodices (cuts of pork) to tripe and drisheen (blood pudding). Toby Simmonds sells 15 or 20 different types of olives. There are breads of every sort, game, chickens, and buttered (preserved) eggs. I love the banter with the stallholders and bring every group of students here because there are foods for sale in that market which would be impossible to get anywhere else in the world.

Above: the hall of the Cookery School is where we greet the students when they first arrive. The chairs are made by my son, Isaac.

Right: the chickens are totally free-range and wander everywhere about the School grounds.

Far right: the Muscovy ducks and the geese are beautiful birds; their purpose is mainly ornamental, but they do keep the snails at bay.

The tiny daffodils burst into flower in the fruit garden, underplanted with spring bulbs to cheer me up in the dreary weeks of February and March. Now we have crocus, *Iris reticulata*, winter snowflakes. The hellebore bed is a triumph. Someone kindly gave me a huge gift token for Carewswood Garden Centre and I blitzed the whole lot on hellebores, 10 or 12 kinds. Fortunately they love that spot under the fruit garden wall, outside the Cookery School window, and we will plant lots of snowdrops in the gaps next year. We have incredibly fragrant little violets, so beautiful and so much a portent of spring, which must have been planted by the Strangmans and which I collected out of the ditches; we make sensationally pretty crystallized violets in the School.

Easter comes and the three-month course, exhausting as it is exhilarating, finishes up with the tension of the exams. The students and the staff go off to well-earned breaks and we celebrate with glorious Easter lamb, served with

Above: the snake's head fritillaria (*Fritillaria meleagris*) has a characteristic freckling, which does not appear on the white form, 'Aphrodite'. At Ballymaloe they contrast beautifully with the miniature daffodils at Eastertime.

Right: the fruit garden is underplanted with many spring flowers; among them various crocuses, tulips and daphnes.

Above: *Vibernum x. Bodnantense* flowers in the very early spring and has the most delicate fragrance. It lasts extremely well as a cut flower and perfumes the entire room.

fresh mint – I use spearmint for the best flavour, though we grow five or six different varieties. There are the decorated eggs and we have picnics – it's in my blood. My mother, Elizabeth O'Connell, once took all nine of her children on a wonderful picnic to the top of Cullohill Mountain on Christmas Day. I make the Simnel cake on Easter Monday and then toast it so it's still fresh on our picnics – divine with cups of Barry's tea. We take sausages and our son Isaac lights a fire and they are cooked in the little black tin pan which has done service for so many years. We picnic at a special place just beside the river Dissour at Easter, where there are beds of wild garlic, and wood anemones are in bloom. Quite magical.

Wild Garlic Soup

SERVES 6

55g (2oz) butter
280g (10oz) potatoes, peeled and
diced
140g (5oz) onions, diced
2 cups chopped wild garlic (bulbs and
leaves)
1 teaspoon salt
Freshly ground black pepper
1.2 litres (2 pints) Home-made Chicken
Stock (see page 184)
About 125ml (4fl oz) cream
or creamy milk

GARNISH
Wild garlic flowers

In late April the air at the top of Wilson's Wood is heavy with the smell of wild garlic. The pretty white flowers mix with the bluebells and primroses. Both the bulbs and leaves of wild garlic or ransoms are used to flavour this delicious soup. Dig the bulbs up, don't pull them. The flowers look divine sprinkled over the top of the bowls of soup.

Melt the butter in a heavy saucepan. When it foams, add the potatoes, onions and wild garlic and toss in the butter until well coated. Sprinkle with salt and pepper. Cover and sweat on a gentle heat for 10 minutes. Add the stock and cook until the vegetables are soft.

Purée the soup in a blender or food processor, then taste and adjust the seasoning. Add a little cream or creamy milk to taste. Serve, sprinkled with a few wild garlic flowers.

Spring Cabbage Soup with Crispy Seaweed

SERVES 6

55g (2oz) butter
140g (5oz) potatoes, chopped
115g (4oz) onions, chopped
Salt and freshly ground black pepper
900ml (1¹/₂ pints) Home-made
Chicken Stock (see page 184)
250g (9oz) spring cabbage leaves (stalks removed), chopped
50–125ml (1¹/₂ –4fl oz) cream or creamy milk

CRISPY SEAWEED
Savoy cabbage (or the outer leaves of Spring cabbage)
Salt
Sugar
Oil for frying

The idea of cabbage soup may not thrill you, but just try this one. Use the freshest, greenest cabbage and take great care not to overcook it. Cook and eat, don't reheat! The Crispy Seaweed may be used as a garnish or served separately, as an appetizer.

Melt the butter in a heavy pan. When it foams, add the potatoes and onions and turn them in the butter until well coated. Sprinkle with salt and pepper. Cover and sweat on a gentle heat for 10 minutes. Add the stock (heat first if you wish to speed things up) and boil until the potatoes are soft. Add the cabbage and cook, uncovered, until the cabbage is just cooked – a matter of 4–5 minutes. Keeping the lid off retains the green colour.

To make the Crispy Seaweed, remove the outer leaves from the cabbage, cut out the stalks, roll the dry leaves into a cigar shape and slice into the thinnest possible shreds with a very sharp knife. Heat the oil in a deep-fryer to 180°C/350°F. Toss in some cabbage and cook for just a few seconds. As soon as it starts to crisp, remove and drain on kitchen paper. Sprinkle with salt and sugar. Toss and serve as a garnish on the soup or just nibble, it's quite addictive – worse than peanuts or popcorn!

Purée the soup in a liquidizer or blender. Taste and adjust the seasoning. Add the cream or creamy milk before serving. Serve alone or with a mound of Crispy Seaweed on top.

Potato, Spring Onion and Tarragon Soup with Crusty Breadsticks

We make this soup with the first fresh tarragon of spring, when the potatoes are beginning to get old. Crusty Breadsticks are delicious with it but of course you can eat them with any soup. The more rustic-looking they are the better.

SERVES 6

Ballymaloe White Yeast Bread Dough (see page 180)
Coarse salt, cumin seeds or freshly chopped rosemary, to sprinkle

SOUP
55g (2oz) butter
425g (15oz) potatoes, peeled and diced
115g (4oz) spring onions (we use both the white and the green parts)
1 teaspoon salt
Freshly ground black pepper
2–3 teaspoons chopped French tarragon
900ml (1¹/₂ pints) Home-made Chicken Stock (see page 184)
125ml (4fl oz) creamy milk

GARNISH
Fresh tarragon

Prepare the dough (see page 180).

Preheat the oven to 230°C/450°F/gas mark 8.

When the dough has been 'knocked back', let it rest for a few minutes. Sprinkle the work surface with coarse salt, cumin seeds or freshly chopped rosemary. Pull off small pieces of dough, each about 15g (¹/₂oz) in weight. Cover the rest of the dough while you work with one piece. Roll each one into a thin breadstick, brush with a tiny drop of oil, then roll the sticks individually in the salt, seeds or herbs until they are well coated. Place on a baking sheet and bake for 10–15 minutes or until golden brown and crisp. Cool on a wire rack. (Breadsticks are usually baked without a final rising but for a slightly lighter result let the shaped dough rise for about 10 minutes before baking.)

Melt the butter in a heavy saucepan. When it foams, add the potatoes and the spring onions and toss them in the butter until well coated. Sprinkle with salt and pepper. Cover and sweat on a gentle heat for 8–10 minutes. Add the chopped tarragon and the stock. Cook until the vegetables are just soft, then purée the soup in a blender. Taste and adjust the seasoning. Thin with creamy milk to the required consistency. Serve sprinkled with a little snipped tarragon.

Carpaccio with Slivers of Parmesan, Rocket and Truffle Oil

SERVES 12

450g (1lb) fillet of beef, preferably Aberdeen Angus (fresh not frozen)
Fresh rocket (arugula), about 5 leaves per person
4–5 very thin slivers Parmesan cheese per person (Parmigiano Reggiano is best)
Sea salt and freshly ground black pepper
Truffle oil or extra virgin olive oil

Many people feel uneasy about eating raw beef but we have no qualms because fortunately we have a butcher who has confidence in his source.

Chill the meat, then slice it as thinly as possible with a very sharp knife. Place each slice on a piece of oiled cling film and cover with another piece of oiled cling film. Roll gently with a rolling pin until it is almost transparent and has doubled in size. Peel the cling film off the top, invert the meat on to a chilled plate, and gently peel away the other piece of cling film.

Put the rocket leaves on top of the beef and scatter very thin slivers of Parmesan over the top of the rocket. Sprinkle with sea salt and pepper. Alternatively pile the beef on top. Drizzle with truffle oil or with very best extra virgin olive oil and serve immediately with crusty bread – ciabatta and Focaccia (see page 178) are best.

Deep-fried Sprats with Aïoli

AIOLI
1–4 cloves garlic, depending on size
Pinch of English mustard or ¼ teaspoon
French mustard
Salt and freshly ground black pepper
2 egg yolks, preferably free-range
230ml (8fl oz) oil (either sunflower,
groundnut, or olive oil: we use 3 parts
groundnut to 1 part olive oil)

1 dessertspoon white wine vinegar

Oil for deep-frying
450g (1lb) sprats
Well-seasoned flour
Lemon segments
Oyster shells (optional) to serve

GARNISH
2 teaspoons chopped parsley

In general January has few highlights, apart from the arrival of the Seville oranges for marmalade. When the sprats arrive in Ballycotton, however, the excitement is tremendous. We feast on them (deep-fried, soused, pickled and smoked) for a few short weeks. We don't even think of gutting them; you may be shocked but we eat them insides and all!

First make the aïoli. Using a pestle and mortar, work the garlic with a little salt and pepper until smooth; then work in the mustard and egg yolks. Add the wine vinegar and the oil drop by drop, stirring constantly with the pestle. Once the sauce has started to thicken, the rest of the oil can be added more quickly. Stir in the chopped parsley.

Alternatively, use a food processor to purée the garlic, mustard, egg yolks and seasoning. With the blades still turning, add the oil in a thin stream. Add the vinegar at the end.

Taste the aïoli and add a few drops of fresh lemon juice, salt and pepper if necessary. Just before serving heat the oil in a deep-fryer to 200°C (400°F). Toss the sprats in well-seasoned flour and cook until crisp and golden. Serve immediately with segments of lemon garnished with parsley. An oyster shell on each plate holds a generous spoonful of aïoli perfectly.

Smoked Irish Salmon with Potato Wafers and Horseradish Sauce

4 large potatoes
Olive oil (or a mixture of olive and sun-
flower oil) for deep-frying
Salt
18 slices smoked Irish salmon
Horseradish Sauce (see page 186)
Freshly squeezed lemon juice
Freshly ground black pepper

GARNISH
Chives
Red onion, sprinkled with vinegar and sugar

I ate this first in a restaurant in California, made with lox and presented as a crisp high pile. The waiters managed to mince around without it toppling!

Scrub the potatoes and cut into very thin slices, preferably using a mandoline. Heat the oil in a deep-fryer and cook the potato slices until crisp and golden. Drain on kitchen paper. Season with salt.

Prepare the Horseradish Sauce.

To assemble: put a little Sauce in the centre of a plate with a warm potato wafer on top and a ruffle of smoked salmon on top of that. Brush with freshly squeezed lemon juice, then add another blob of Sauce, some pepper and another potato wafer. Repeat twice more if you can manage to balance it, ending with a potato wafer. Garnish with more Horseradish Sauce, red onion rings and a couple of cheeky chives.

Warm Salad of Lambs' Kidneys, Straw Potatoes and Caramelized Shallots

SERVES 4

About 4 generous handfuls of a selection of salad leaves (butterhead, lollo rosso, curly endive, cos, watercress, rocket etc.)

FOR THE DRESSING
6 tablespoons olive oil
2 tablespoons white wine vinegar
1/4 teaspoon Dijon mustard
Salt and freshly ground black pepper
A pinch sugar

20 Caramelized Shallots (see below)

FOR THE STRAW POTATOES
1 large potato (115–175g/4–6oz)
Oil for deep-frying

2 tablespoons olive oil
4 lambs' kidneys, trimmed of all fat and gristle and cut into 1cm (1/2in) dice
Salt and freshly ground black pepper
1 tablespoon freshly chopped marjoram

GARNISH
Majoram sprigs

The offal of spring lamb is so tender. We feast on lamb's kidneys when the lambs are young. Our butcher, Mr Cuddigan, keeps his own herd on herb-filled pastures with delicious results.

Wash and dry the salad leaves, tear into bite-sized pieces and keep in a salad bowl. Whisk together the ingredients for the dressing and set aside. Prepare and cook the Caramelized Shallots.

Peel the potato and cut into fine julienne strips on a mandoline, in a food processor or by hand. Wash off excess starch with cold water, drain and pat dry. Preheat the oil in a deep-fryer to 200°C (400°F). Fry the potatoes until golden brown and crispy. Keep them warm to serve with the salad.

Just before serving heat the olive oil in a frying pan until very hot. Season the kidneys with salt and pepper, add to the pan and cook according to your preference. Sprinkle with chopped marjoram. Don't overcook them or they will become tough and rubbery. While the kidneys are cooking, toss the lettuce leaves quickly with the dressing and divide between the plates. Put the warm shallots around each pile of salad and arrange the Straw Potatoes carefully on top of each shallot in a little pile. Finally, sprinkle the cooked kidneys straight from the pan on to the salads. Garnish with tiny sprigs of majoram and serve immediately.

Caramelized Shallots

SERVES 4

450g (1lb) peeled shallots
55g (2oz) butter
125ml (4fl oz) water
1–2 tablespoons sugar
Salt and freshly ground black pepper
Sprig of thyme or rosemary

Serve these with Warm Salad of Lambs' Kidneys (see above), steaks, fish or a mixture of roasted vegetables (see page 169).

Put all of the ingredients into a saucepan. Bring to the boil and simmer, covered, until the shallots are almost tender. Remove the lid and allow the juices to evaporate. Watch and turn carefully as the shallots begin to caramelize.

Green Asparagus on Buttered Toast

SERVES 4

16–20 fresh asparagus spears
4 slices of very fresh bread, preferably Ballymaloe White Yeast Bread (see page 180)
Butter

Hollandaise Sauce (see page 182)

GARNISH
Freshly chopped chervil

Of all the ways I have eaten asparagus, this is my absolute favourite.

Peel and trim the root-end of the asparagus. Save the trimmings for soup.

Make the Hollandaise Sauce and keep warm.

Just before serving, cook the asparagus in boiling salted water. If you have a special asparagus kettle that's wonderful but you can manage very well without one. Depending upon the thickness of the spears, the asparagus may take up to 4–8 minutes to cook. Test by putting the tip of a sharp knife through the thicker end; it should go through easily. Remove the spears from the water and drain.

Toast the bread slices and butter them while they are still warm. Cut off the crusts if you must, but the bread is so good that I leave them on. Divide the asparagus between the slices and top with a few spoonfuls of Hollandaise. Garnish with freshly chopped chervil and eat immediately.

Goat's Cheese Crostini with Balsamic Onions and Watercress

SERVES 4

150g (6 oz) fresh goat's cheese
Salt and freshly ground black pepper
125 ml (4 fl oz) softly whipped cream
1/2 teaspoon chopped thyme
1/4 teaspoon chopped rosemary
2 tablespoons olive oil
350g (12oz) sliced onions
Balsamic vinegar

Bunch of watercress, trimmed and washed

FOR THE CROSTINI
4 slices white country bread, or 8 slices ciabatta or French baguette cut at an angle
Extra virgin olive oil

Our goat's cheese comes from a herd owned by Erwin and Ina Korner near Youghal, in County Cork. The goats live a very happy life. The cheese made from their milk is soft so try to find an equivalent, very fresh, goat's cheese for this recipe.

Sieve the goat's cheese into a bowl, season with salt and pepper and fold in the softly whipped cream and chopped herbs. Cover and refrigerate until needed. Heat one tablespoon of olive oil in a sauté pan. Toss in the sliced onions and sweat until almost soft and lightly caramelized. Add the balsamic vinegar, cook for 2–3 minutes and set aside.

Heat enough olive oil to cover the base of a frying pan to a depth of 2.5cm (1in) until the oil is almost smoking. Cook the bread on both sides until pale golden. Drain on kitchen paper.

Preheat the grill or a hot oven and spread a generous amount of goat's cheese cream on the crostini and pop under the grill or into the oven. Strip the watercress leaves from the main stalks and toss the leaves in a little extra virgin olive oil and a few drops of balsamic vinegar. Season with salt and pepper. Put the crostini on a bed of watercress, with a few balsamic onion rings sprinkled round the edge. Serve immediately.

Char-grilled Scallops with Aubergines and Pesto

SERVES 4

1–2 aubergines
Salt and freshly ground black pepper
Pesto (see page 186)
Olive oil
12–16 scallops

GARNISH
Fresh basil leaves

I tasted this combination in Cantina, a restaurant in London, and I was so excited that I wrote about it for the Irish Times *when I got back home. We get our scallops from Kenmare Bay, but wherever you get yours make sure that they are big, plump and sweet.*

Slice the aubergines lengthwise into 5mm ($^1/_4$ in) thick slices, sprinkle with salt and leave to degorge for 15–20 minutes.

Meanwhile make the Pesto (or use a jar of good-quality, ready-made Pesto). Wash the aubergine slices and pat dry with kitchen paper. Brush with a little olive oil and, on a char-grill or a very hot pan-grill, cook quickly on both sides. Just before serving, season the scallops with salt and freshly ground pepper. Cook on the char-grill or pan-grill. (A non-stick pan also gives a very good result.) Allow them to brown well on one side before turning them over.

To serve cover the base of each plate with aubergine slices, arrange three or four scallops and their coral on top and drizzle a little Pesto between the scallops and aubergine slices. Garnish with a sprig of fresh basil and serve immediately.

Pan-fried Scallops with Beurre Blanc

SERVES 4 (OR 8 AS A STARTER)

12 large scallops
Salt and freshly ground black pepper

BEURRE BLANC
3 tablespoons white wine
3 tablespoons white wine vinegar
1 tablespoon shallots, finely chopped
Salt and freshly ground white pepper
1 generous tablespoon cream
175g (6oz) cold unsalted
butter, cut into small cubes
Freshly squeezed lemon juice

GARNISH
Fresh fennel or chervil sprigs

YOU WILL NEED
A non-stick pan

This is the most exquisite way to eat really fresh scallops. Some people may feel beurre blanc appears everywhere these days but this is still the most sublime combination of flavours.

First make the Beurre Blanc. Put the wine, wine vinegar, shallots and pepper into a heavy-bottomed stainless-steel saucepan and reduce down to about 1/2 tablespoon. Add the cream and boil again until it thickens. Whisk in the cold butter in little pieces, keeping the sauce just warm enough to absorb the butter. Strain out the shallots, season with salt, white pepper and lemon juice and keep warm in a bowl over hot but not simmering water.

Just before serving, slice the white part of each scallop in half to get two rounds of equal thickness; keep the coral intact. Dry on kitchen paper. Just before cooking, season the scallops with salt and pepper. Heat a non-stick pan and put the scallops directly into it in a single layer, not too close together. Cook on one side until golden before turning over to cook the other side.

Spoon a little very thin Beurre Blanc on to a large hot plate for each person (thin the sauce if necessary by whisking in warm water), arrange the slices of scallop and coral on top of the sauce, garnish with fennel or chervil and serve immediately.

Sea Bass with Asparagus and Fennel

SERVES 6

6 x 175g (6oz) fillets sea bass, scaled but not skinned
Sea salt and freshly ground white pepper
12 fresh asparagus spears
Extra virgin olive oil
1 fennel bulb, trimmed and cut into diagonal slices
Colonna Granverde (lemon-flavoured olive oil)

GARNISH
Fennel leaves

Try to dovetail the cooking of the asparagus, fresh fish and fennel so that everything is ready to serve pretty much at the same moment.

Preheat the oven to 230°C/450°F/gas mark 8; preheat a char-grill or grill pan.

Trim the asparagus and peel the root end thinly with a swivel-top peeler. Drizzle with a little extra virgin olive oil, toss gently to coat, season with sea salt and roast in the preheated oven for 8–10 minutes.

Score the fillets quite deeply on the skin-side to stop them curling. Season with salt and pepper. Heat a thin film of olive oil in a non-stick pan to just below smoking point and place the fillets skin-side down in the pan for 2–3 minutes, until a nice crust forms. Turn the fillets over and complete cooking in the preheated oven – about 5–8 minutes, depending on their thickness.

Drizzle the fennel with extra virgin olive oil and turn gently to coat. Season with salt and pepper. Cook for 1–2 minutes on both sides on the hot grill.

Arrange each fillet of fish skin-side up on a hot plate, drizzle a little Colonna Granverde over the fish. Surround each plate with the roast asparagus cut into smaller pieces at an angle and slices of char-grilled fennel. Garnish with a few feathery fennel leaves and eat immediately.

Wild Irish Salmon with Seakale

SERVES 6

1.1kg (2½lb) centre cut of fresh wild Irish salmon
Salt (use a generous tablespoon to every 1.2 litres (2 pints) of water)
Water for poaching

Hollandaise Sauce (see page 182)

Seakale (see page 38)

GARNISH
Fennel leaves

Salmon and seakale and Hollandaise Sauce – a marriage made in heaven. But if a small piece of fish is cooked in a large amount of water, much of the flavour will escape into the water, so I use the smallest pan possible. Needless to say I never poach a salmon cutlet because the maximum surface is exposed to the water, resulting in maximum loss of flavour.

First poach the salmon. The proportion of salt to water is very important. The fish should be covered, but aim to use the minimum amount of water to preserve maximum flavour. Choose a pan which will fit the fish exactly. Half fill the pan with the measured salt water and bring to the boil. Put in the fish, cover, bring back to the boil and simmer gently for 20 minutes. Turn off the heat and allow the fish to sit in the water for no longer than 5–8 minutes. Meanwhile make the Hollandaise Sauce and cook the seakale.

Remove the fish from the poaching liquid, remove the skin and divide the fish into portions, being careful to remove all bones. Garnish with fennel leaves and serve hot with the sauce, seakale and some new potatoes.

Roast Cod, Hake, or Grey Sea Mullet with Crispy Onions and Parsley Pesto

SERVES 6

Tomato Fondue (see page 182)
Parsley Pesto (see page 186)
Crispy Onions (see page 188)
6 x 175g (6oz) fillets of cod, hake, or
grey sea mullet with skin on
Extra virgin olive oil
Salt and freshly ground white pepper

GARNISH

Flat-leaf parsley or chervil leaves

For this recipe you need to use a round fish with a thick fillet. It is vital to leave the skin on and to use fresh fish.

Preheat the oven to 230°C/450°F/gas mark 8.

Prepare the Tomato Fondue, Parsley Pesto and Crispy Onions.

Score the fish skin quite deeply to prevent it from curling. Heat a thin film of extra virgin olive oil in a non-stick pan to just before smoking point. Season the fillets and place skin-side down in the pan until a nice crust forms. Turn the fillets over and complete cooking skin-side up in the oven.

To serve put a piece of roast fish skin-side uppermost on a hot plate. Garnish the plate with two dollops each of Tomato Fondue, Parsley Pesto and Crispy Onions. Sprinkle with flat leaf parsley or chervil leaves. Drizzle with extra virgin olive oil and serve immediately because the skin loses its crispness quite quickly.

Deh-Ta Hsiung's Steamed Grey Sea Mullet

SERVES ABOUT 6

1 grey sea mullet (sea bass could be used instead), scaled, trimmed and cleaned

1 teaspoon salt

1 teaspoon sesame seed oil

4 spring onions

2–3 dried mushrooms, soaked and thinly shredded

55g (2oz) pork fillet or cooked ham, thinly shredded

2 tablespoons light soy sauce

1 tablespoon rice wine or sherry

5cm (1½in) peeled ginger root, thinly shredded

2 tablespoons sunflower oil

We first invited Deh-Ta, an inspirational Chinese chef, to come and teach at the School in 1984. He adored Ireland and the flavour of grey sea mullet was almost enough to tempt him to move to Ireland. Grey sea mullet is every bit as good as sea bass but at a fraction of the price.

Wash the fish under the cold tap and dry well, inside and out, with kitchen paper. Slash both sides of the fish diagonally as far as the bone at 12mm (½in) intervals with a sharp knife. Rub half the salt and all the sesame seed oil inside the fish, and place it on 2–3 spring onions in an oval dish. Mix the mushrooms and pork or ham with the remaining salt, a little of the soy sauce and the rice wine or sherry. Stuff the fish with half the mixture. Put the rest on top with the ginger. Place in a hot steamer. Steam vigorously for 15 minutes.

Meanwhile, shred the remaining spring onion thinly. Heat the sunflower oil in a little saucepan until bubbling. Remove the fish dish from the steamer, arrange the spring onion shreds on top, pour over the remaining soy sauce and then the hot oil, from head to tail. Serve hot.

Baked Trout with Spinach Butter Sauce

SERVES 4

2 x 900g (2lb) rainbow trout, whole
25–55g (1–2oz) butter
Salt and freshly ground pepper
Sprig of fennel

SPINACH BUTTER SAUCE

85g (3oz) spinach leaves
150ml (5fl oz) cream
85g (3oz) butter
Water if necessary

YOU WILL NEED

Tin foil

We can sometimes get lovely fat pink trout about 2 years old which have a wonderful taste – much better than the smaller ones. This is a horrendously rich-sounding sauce but it's delicious and the flavour is sublime.

Preheat the oven to 190°C/375°F/gas mark 5.

Gut the trout and wash well making sure to remove the line of blood from the inside near the back bone, dry with kitchen paper, season inside and out with salt and freshly ground pepper. Put a blob of butter and a sprig of fennel into the centre of each trout. Take a large sheet of tin foil, smear a little butter on the centre, put the trout onto the buttered bit and fold over the edges into a papillotte shape. Seal well to ensure that none of the juices can escape. Repeat with the other trout. Put the two tin foil parcels on a baking tray but make sure they are not touching. Bake in the pre-heated oven for about 30 minutes.

Meanwhile make the Spinach Butter Sauce. Remove stalks from the spinach, wash and cook in 600ml (1 pint) salted boiling water. Cook for 4–5 minutes or until just soft and tender, drain. Press out every last drop of water and chop finely. Put the cream into a saucepan and simmer on a gentle heat until reduced to about 3 tablespoons or until it is in danger of burning. Then, on a very low heat, whisk in the butter bit by bit as though you were making a Hollandaise Sauce. Stir in the spinach.

When the fish is cooked, open the parcels and use some of the delicious juices to thin the sauce. Put the two parcels on to a hot serving dish and bring to the table. Skin the fish and lift the juicy pink flesh on to hot plates. Spoon the spinach butter sauce over the fish and eat immediately.

Chicken with Morels

SERVES 4–6

1 free-range chicken, 1.5kg (3¹/₂ lb) in weight
Salt and freshly ground black pepper
25g (1oz) unsalted butter
350ml (12 fl oz) Chardonnay or Meursault
6 cloves garlic, unpeeled
1 bouquet garni (with a good few parsley stalks, a sprig of thyme, a sprig of tarragon and a scrap of bay leaf)
55g (2oz) dry morels or 115g (4oz) trimmed fresh morels
140–230ml (5–8fl oz) Home-made Chicken Stock (see page 184) for soaking dry morels
230ml (8fl oz) cream
A little Roux (see page 182)

GARNISH
Sprigs of flat leaf parsley

Morels start to appear in the woods from about St Patrick's Day – mid-March onwards. People are notoriously secretive about their sources, not surprisingly. When you are choosing fresh morels they should have a very heavy perfume. Use as many as you can find or afford; in this recipe 55g (2oz) alone will perfume the sauce deliciously but 225g (8oz) would be even better. Dried morels should be kept in a sealed, dry jar. Always buy the best you can afford and try not to buy more than you need.

Preheat the oven to 180°C/350°F/gas mark 4.

Season the cavity and breast of the chicken with salt and pepper. Smear the butter over the breast and legs. Put into a flameproof casserole with the wine, unpeeled garlic and bouquet garni. Bring to the boil on top of the stove, cover and transfer to the preheated oven for 1¹/₄–1¹/₂ hours, depending on the size of the chicken. If the morels are dry, cover with boiling chicken stock and leave to soak for an hour.

As soon as the chicken is cooked, transfer to a carving dish and keep warm. Skim the fat from the pan juices with a metal spoon, and remove the garlic and bouquet garni. Add the cream, bring to the boil and thicken by reduction (or, better still, whisk in just a little roux). If the morels are fresh, wash them carefully to remove all traces of grit or soil. Melt a little butter in a hot pan, and toss the morels gently for 2–3 minutes. Season with salt and pepper. Add the morels (and their soaking liquid, if using dried ones) to the sauce. Simmer gently for 5 minutes. Meanwhile carve the chicken and arrange on a serving dish. Taste the sauce and season if necessary, spoon the sauce over and divide the morels equally between each helping. Garnish simply with a little flat-leaf parsley and serve immediately.

Easter Lamb with Roast Spring Onions

SERVES 6–8

1 leg of spring lamb
Salt and freshly ground black pepper
12–18 spring onions, trimmed

GRAVY
600ml (1 pint) lamb stock or Home-made
Chicken Stock (see page 184)
A little Roux (see page 182)
Salt and freshly ground black pepper

Mint Sauce (see page 188)

GARNISH
Sprigs of mint and parsley

Young spring lamb is sweet and succulent and needs absolutely no embellishment apart from a dusting of salt and pepper and a little fresh Mint Sauce, made from the first tender sprigs of mint from the cold frame in the kitchen garden. I have a standing order with Mr Cuddigan from one year to the next for spring lamb. For me this is the quintessential taste of Easter. The first mint of the year only just appears in our garden only just in time for Easter and when the festival is very early it's touch and go as to whether we will have enough for Mint Sauce.

Preheat the oven to 180°C/350°F/gas mark 4.

If possible ask your butcher to remove the aitch bone from the top of the leg of lamb so that it will be easier to carve later, then trim the knuckle end of the leg. Season the skin with salt and pepper. Put into a roasting tin and roast in the preheated oven for about 1–1¼ hours for rare meat, 1¼–1½ hours for medium and 1½–2 hours for well done, depending on size. Pop in the spring onions for the last 20 minutes or so.

Test the lamb with a skewer When the lamb is cooked to your taste, remove the joint and the onions to a carving dish. Leave the meat to rest for 10 minutes before carving.

Meanwhile make the gravy. Remove the fat from the juices in the roasting tin with a metal spoon and add the stock. Bring to the boil and whisk in a little roux to thicken slightly. Taste and allow to bubble up until the flavour is concentrated enough. Correct the seasoning and serve the gravy with the garnished lamb, mint sauce, spring onions and lots of crusty roast potatoes.

Risotto with Broad Beans, Peas, Green Asparagus and Sugar Snaps

SERVES 8

225g (8oz) broad beans
Salt and freshly ground black pepper
115g (4oz) sugar snaps
6 stalks green asparagus
225g (8oz) peas
1.7–2 litres (3–3½ pints) Home-made Chicken Stock (see page 184)
40g (1½oz) butter
115g (4oz) onions, finely chopped
400g (14oz) Carnaroli, Vilano, Nano or Arborio rice
90ml (3fl oz) dry white wine
25g (1oz) Parmesan (Parmigiano Reggiano), freshly grated, plus extra for serving

I like my risottos to be soft and soupy. Make sure that the vegetables you use for this dish are fresh and have enough green colour. We make this at the end of spring when the first of the crop are coming up in the vegetable garden and greenhouse.

Bring 600ml (1 pint) water to the boil in a saucepan, add the broad beans and salt and cook for 2–3 minutes, or until almost tender. Drain and refresh in cold water. Slip the beans out of their shells.

Meanwhile, cook the sugar snaps, again in boiling salted water, until *al dente*, then cook the asparagus for just 4–5 minutes. Cook the peas for 3–4 minutes. If you can keep your eye on several pots at the same time, do all this while cooking the risotto.

To start the risotto, bring the chicken stock to the boil at the back of the cooker and keep at a low simmer. Melt 25g (1oz) of the butter in a large saucepan, add the finely chopped onion and cook over a medium heat until soft but not coloured, then add the rice and a generous pinch of salt. Stir the rice over the heat for 2–3 minutes or until it turns translucent, then increase the heat and add the dry white wine.

When the wine has evaporated, add a couple of ladles of stock, stir and reduce the heat to medium; keep stirring. When the liquid has almost been absorbed, add another ladleful, stirring all the time. After about 10 minutes, add the beans, peas and sugar snaps. Continue to ladle in more stock until it is absorbed. After about 5 minutes, taste the rice: it should be just cooked. Stir in the remaining butter, the freshly grated Parmesan and the asparagus – cut at an angle in 2.5cm (1in) pieces. Add a little more stock if necessary – the risotto should be moist. Taste and correct the seasoning.

Serve immediately in hot bowls with extra freshly grated Parmesan as required to sprinkle over the top.

Seakale with Melted Butter

450g (1lb) seakale
55–85g (2–3oz) butter
Salt and freshly ground black pepper

We grow seakale in the herb garden and in the kitchen garden – it is rarely found in shops so it is really worth trying to find a space in your garden or flower bed. You will need chimney liners or plastic buckets or, in an ideal world, terracotta seakale pots, to blanch the kale from November to April. I've got lots of pots made by the Whichford Pottery. I was so sorely tempted when I saw them at the Chelsea Flower Show, that I went on a mighty spree and had to hide the evidence from Timmy for ages!

Wash the seakale gently and trim into manageable lengths – about 10cm (4in). Bring about 600ml (1 pint) of water to a fast rolling boil, and add a generous $^1/_2$ teaspoon of salt. Pop in the seakale, cover and boil until tender – 5–15 minutes, depending on the thickness.

Just as soon as a knife pierces the seakale easily, drain it and then serve on hot plates with a little melted butter and perhaps a few small triangles of toast. At the beginning of its short season in April, we eat it on hot toast with melted butter or Hollandaise Sauce. When the kale becomes more abundant it makes a wonderful accompaniment to fish, particularly Wild Irish Salmon (see page 30) or sea trout.

Cardoons Layered with Parmesan

1.8kg (4lb) cardoons, trimmed
Water acidulated with the juice of a lemon
Butter
Salt and freshly ground black pepper
Parmesan cheese (Parmigiano Reggiano is the best), freshly grated
Cream

Cardoons bring to mind one of the 'Two Fat Ladies', Clarissa Dickson-Wright, who almost single-handedly brought cardoons into the limelight. They look very like their cousins, the globe artichokes, but are cultivated for their stalks, not their thistle-like flowers. We have been growing them for about a decade now.

Preheat the oven to 200°C/400°F/gas mark 6.

Separate the cardoon stalks from the hearts. Save the tender hearts for eating raw , if you like. Cut the stalks into manageable lengths, 7.5–10cm (3–4in) and cook in acidulated water for 30–35 minutes. Drain and refresh in cold water; remove the strings from the outer stalks.

Smear a lasagne dish with butter and arrange a layer of cardoons in the base. Dot with butter, season with salt and pepper, and sprinkle with freshly grated Parmesan, then another layer of cardoons, butter, more seasoning and Parmesan. Continue adding layers until the dish is full, finishing with a layer of cardoons. Pour on a little cream and sprinkle the top with Parmesan cheese. Bake in the preheated oven for 15–20 minutes or until the cardoons are tender and the top is bubbling and golden.

Cottier's Kale

SERVES 6

1.35kg (3lb) cottiers kale
1.8 litres (3 pints) water
1½ teaspoons salt
25–55g (1–2oz) butter
Salt and freshly ground black pepper

One of the most treasured vegetables in our garden is a very ancient type of perennial kale. Brassica oleracea is thought to be about 2,000 years old and is of tremendous interest to botanists. Locally it may be called 'cut and come', 'cottiers kale', 'winter greens' or, most appropriate of all, 'hungry gap' , which refers to the fact that this humble, everlasting kale is the only green vegetable to cheer and nourish during the barren period between winter and early spring when nothing is ready to harvest. You can't just buy a packet of seeds; you will have to grow it from a slip or cutting. A few years ago I came across it in the eighteenth-century walled garden at Glin Castle in County Limerick. The gardener, Tom Wall, gave me a few slips which I popped into our vegetable garden. That real treasure has increased and multiplied and every year from late winter to early spring it produces a wealth of tender greens and, true to its local name, the more one cuts the more it comes. It has the flavour of kale but the melting texture of spinach.

Trim the stalks and wash the kale. Bring the water to a fast rolling boil in a saucepan, add the salt and kale. Cook uncovered for about 25 minutes or until tender. Drain off all the water and season well with salt and pepper. Chop well and beat in a really generous lump of butter. Taste and adjust the seasoning if you need to.

Braised White Turnips with Annual Marjoram

SERVES 4–6

450g (1lb) small white turnips
12–25g (¹/₂-1oz) butter
1-2 tablespoons chopped annual marjoram
or oregano, but reserve
a couple of sprigs
Salt and freshly ground white pepper

These turnips are best in the late spring when they just fit in the palm of the hand. This recipe is sensational on its own but particularly delicious with duck and lamb. Don't throw away the turnip tops but save them for wilted greens or soup.

Wash and peel the white turnips. Quarter or thickly slice the turnips. Melt the butter in a flameproof casserole amd toss the turnip until it is barely coated. Season with salt and pepper. Add no more than a tablespoon of water and a couple of sprigs of annual marjoram or oregano. Cover with a butter wrapper or a piece of greaseproof paper and the casserole lid. Cook over a low heat for 8–10 minutes until the turnip is just tender. Remove the cooked sprigs and add a little freshly chopped marjoram. Taste, correct the seasoning and serve.

Scallion Champ

SERVES 4–6

6–8 unpeeled 'old' potatoes eg Kerrs Pinks
or Golden Wonder
55–110g (2–4oz) finely chopped
spring onions
300–350ml (10–12fl oz) milk
55–115g (2–4oz) butter
Salt and freshly ground black pepper

A bowl of mashed potatoes flecked with green spring onions (scallions) and a knob of butter melting in the centre is 'comfort' food at its best.

Scrub the potatoes and boil them in their jackets. Cover the sping onions with cold milk and bring slowly to the boil. Simmer for about 3–4 minutes, then turn off the heat and leave to infuse. Peel and mash the potatoes while hot, mix with the boiling milk and spring onions. Beat in half the butter. Season to taste with salt and freshly ground pepper. Serve in a large bowl with the remaining butter melting in the centre.

You can reheat the 'champ' later in a moderate oven (180°C/350°F/gas mark 4). Cover with foil while it reheats to avoid a crust forming on the top.

Spring Creams with Green Gooseberry and Elderflower Compote

SERVES 6–8

SPRING CREAMS
600ml (1 pint) double cream
1–2 vanilla pods, split lengthways
55g (2oz) caster sugar
Scant 2 teaspoons powdered gelatine
2 tablespoons water

GOOSEBERRY AND ELDERFLOWER COMPOTE
900g (2lb) green gooseberries
2–3 elderflower heads
450g (1lb) granulated sugar
600ml (1 pint) water

DECORATION
Gooseberry leaves (optional)
Softly whipped cream
Barbados sugar

6–8 moulds (90–125ml/3–4fl oz capacity) lightly brushed with non-scented oil – sunflower or groundnut

In May the whole of the Irish countryside is full of elder blooms. We used to be nervous of the tree as children because there is an old Irish saying that if you hit someone with an elder twig they will not grow any taller. But now as soon as we see the flowers we rush out to the fruit garden to check the size of the gooseberries. I would love to congratulate the first person who thought of combining these two ingredients. When they cook together the muscat flavour of the elder blossoms balances the tartness of the gooseberries magically. Eat it on its own, with ice-cream, with carrageen moss pudding, or with these delectable Spring Creams which are completely exquisite when made with our rich Irish Cream.

First make the Spring Creams. Put the cream into a heavy-bottomed saucepan with the split vanilla pods and caster sugar. Put on a low heat and bring to the shivery stage.

Meanwhile, 'sponge' the gelatine in the water. Put the bowl in a saucepan of simmering water until the gelatine is dissolved. Add a little of the cream to the gelatine, then stir both mixtures together. Remove the vanilla pods and then pour into the moulds. When cold, cover and refrigerate until set, preferably overnight.

Next make the compote. Top and tail the gooseberries. Tie the elderflower heads in a little square of muslin, put in a stainless steel or enamelled saucepan, add the sugar and cover with the water. Bring to the boil gently and simmer slowly for 2 minutes. Add the gooseberries and simmer just until the fruit bursts. Leave to get cold then remove the elderflowers.

To serve: put a large gooseberry leaf on a plate. Turn out a wobbly Spring Cream carefully on to or beside the leaf and spoon a little of the compote on to the plate. Put a blob of softly whipped cream to the side. Sprinkle this with the Barbados sugar and serve immediately.

Semi-freddo di Mandorle

SERVES 20–25

PRALINE
100g (3¹/₂oz) caster sugar
100g (3¹/₂oz) unskinned almonds

500ml (17fl oz) double cream
100g (3¹/₂oz) caster sugar

5 free-range eggs, separated
55g (2oz) caster sugar

DECORATION
Extra praline: 115g (4oz) caster sugar
115g (4oz) unskinned almonds

YOU WILL NEED
2 loaf tins
cling film

This exquisite dinner-party dessert comes from Erice in Sicily. It is very easy to make but as ever its flavour depends on having really good-quality ingredients. It is also delicious served with bitter chocolate sauce or with fresh raspberries, loganberries or mulberries in late summer. It is truly superb with the Kumquat Compote on page 173.

First make the praline. Put the sugar and unskinned almonds into a heavy-bottomed sauté pan over a low heat until the sugar gradually melts and turns to a rich caramel colour, do not stir. When the sugar has caramelized and not before, carefully rotate the pan until the nuts are all covered with caramel. When the nuts go 'pop', pour the praline on to a lightly oiled Swiss roll tin or oiled marble slab. Leave to get quite cold. When the praline is quite hard, crush in a food processor or with a rolling pin: the texture should be quite coarse and gritty.

Meanwhile whisk the chilled cream with the sugar until softly whipped. Cover and keep in the refrigerator until needed. Whisk the egg yolks with the sugar until light and fluffy, then fold in the whipped cream very delicately. Fold the crushed praline into the mousse. Whisk the egg whites stiffly and fold gently little by little into the mixture. Divide between two loaf tins lined with cling film, cover and freeze for a minimum of 3 hours or a maximum of one month.

Meanwhile make some more praline as before, grind coarsely and set aside.

To serve: cut the Semi-freddo into slices no more than 1cm (¹/₂in) thick, sprinkle a layer of finely crushed praline over each slice. Serve immediately on chilled plates.

February Citrus Fruit Salad

SERVES ABOUT 6

225g (8oz) kumquats
200g (7oz) sugar
350ml (12fl oz) water
1 lime
115–225g (4–8oz) tangerines or
mandarines
225g (8oz) clementines
1 pink grapefruit
2 blood oranges
Lemon juice to taste, if necessary

In the winter when many fruits have abysmal flavour, the citrus fruits are at their best. This delicious, fresh-tasting salad uses a wide variety of the ever-expanding citrus family. It's particularly good when a few blood oranges are included. Ugli fruit, pomelo, tangelos and sweeties all add excitement and zingy flavour. This is a great palate cleaner after a heavy winter meal.

Slice the kumquats into 5mm (¼in) rounds and remove the pips. Dissolve the sugar in the water over a low heat and add the sliced kumquats. Cover and simmer for about 30 minutes or until tender. Remove from the heat. Leave to cool.

Meanwhile, remove the zest from the lime with a zester and add with its juice to the kumquats. Peel the tangerines or mandarines and clementines and remove as much of the white pith and strings as possible. Cut into rounds of 5mm (¼in) thickness, add to the syrup. Segment the pink grapefruit and blood oranges and add to the syrup too. Leave to macerate for at least an hour. Taste and add a squeeze of lemon juice if necessary.

If the juice is too intense, simply dilute with a little cold water or add some more freshly squeezed blood orange juice to taste. Serve chilled.

Fresh Lemon Ice-cream with Crystallized Lemon Peel

SERVES 4

1 free-range egg, separated
250ml (8½fl oz) milk
140g (5oz) caster sugar
Zest and juice of 1 good lemon

DECORATION
Crystallized lemon peel (see page 189)
Fresh mint leaves and borage flowers

This is a fresh tangy light ice-cream, really simple to make and a delight to eat at the end of any meal.

Whisk the egg yolk with the milk. Gradually mix in the sugar. Grate the zest from the lemon carefully on the finest part of a stainless steel grater. Squeeze the juice from the lemon and add with the zest to the liquid. Whisk the egg white until quite stiff and fold into the other ingredients. Freeze in a sorbetière according to the manufacturer's instructions (see also note on sorbetières in recipe for Blackcurrant Leaf Sorbet, page 46). Alternatively, put into a freezer in a covered plastic container.

When the mixture starts to freeze, remove from the freezer and whisk again, or break up in a food processor. Then put it back in the freezer until it is completely frozen. Meanwhile, chill the serving plates.

To serve: scoop the ice-cream into curls and arrange on the chilled plates or in pretty frosted glass dishes. Decorate with crystallized lemon peel, borage flowers and fresh mint leaves if you have them.

Blackcurrant Leaf Sorbet

SERVES ABOUT 6

2 large handfuls of young blackcurrant
leaves
600ml (1 pint) water
225g (8oz) granulated sugar
Juice of 3 freshly squeezed lemons
1 egg white (if you do not have an ice-
cream maker or sorbetière)

This is a very early spring recipe. I watch excitedly as the little black-currant leaves unfurl on the bush outside the School's dining-room window. The strong taste of the leaves foretells the taste of the summer to come and is so welcome at this time of the year. We also adapt this recipe to make elderflower sorbet. Just substitute the blackcurrant leaves with four or five blooming heads of elderflower.

Crush the blackcurrant leaves tightly in your hand then put them into a stainless steel saucepan with the water and sugar. Stir to dissolve the sugar and bring to the boil slowly. Simmer for 2–3 minutes, then set aside to cool completely.* Add the lemon juice and strain and freeze for 20–25 minutes in an ice-cream maker or sorbetière. Serve in chilled glasses or bowls lined with blackcurrant leaves.

Note: If you do not have a sorbetière, simply freeze the sorbet in a dish in the freezer; when it is semi-frozen, whisk until smooth and return to the freezer. Whisk again when almost frozen and fold in the stiffly beaten egg white. Keep in the freezer until required. If you have a food processor, freeze the sorbet completely in a tray then break it up and give it a whizz for a few seconds in the processor, add 1 slightly beaten egg white, whizz again and return to the freezer.

Rhubarb Bread and Butter Pudding

SERVES 6–8

450g (1lb) red rhubarb
Sugar
55g (2oz) butter, preferably unsalted
12 slices good-quality white bread, crusts
removed
450ml (16fl oz) cream
230ml (8fl oz) milk
4 large free-range eggs, beaten lightly
1 teaspoon pure vanilla essence
175g (6oz) sugar
1 tablespoon sugar, for sprinkling on top of
the pudding

My brother Rory O'Connell introduced me to this fantastic combination which then fired my imagination and many experiments have followed. We have been having fun ringing the changes with this recipe. Bread and Butter Pudding is also delicious with apple and cinnamon or even mixed spice. I can't wait to try gooseberry and elderflower as soon as they come back into season. Don't cut down on the cream in this recipe and don't use too much bread.

Cut the rhubarb into 2.5cm (1in) pieces. Put into a dish and sprinkle with sugar. Leave to macerate for an hour.

Butter the bread and arrange four slices, butter-side down, in one layer in the buttered dish. Scatter half the rhubarb over the bread, and cover with another layer of bread, butter-side down. Scatter the remaining rhubarb on top and cover with the remaining bread, buttered side down.

DECORATION
Softly whipped cream

YOU WILL NEED
1 x 20cm (8in) ovenproof pottery
or china dish
A bain-marie or shallow roasting dish

Whisk together the cream, milk, eggs, vanilla essence and sugar in a bowl. Pour the mixture through a fine sieve over the bread. Sprinkle the sugar over the top and let the mixture stand, covered loosely, for at least 1 hour or refrigerate overnight.

Preheat the oven to 180°C/350°F/gas mark 4.

Bake in a bain-marie – the water should be boiling and come halfway up the sides of the baking dish – in the middle of the preheated oven, for about 1 hour or until the top is crisp and golden. Serve the pudding warm with some softly whipped cream.

Lydia's Almond Cake with Crystallized Violets and Angelica

SERVES 10

CRYSTALLIZED VIOLETS
Caster sugar
1 free-range egg white
Freshly picked, sweet-smelling violets

CAKE
115g (4oz) ground almonds
115g (4oz) icing sugar
85g (3oz) plain white flour
3 free-range egg yolks
125ml (4fl oz) melted butter

ICING
175g (6oz) icing sugar
1¹/₂ tablespoons boiling water

Angelica

YOU WILL NEED
A child's clean paintbrush
Baking parchment
18cm (7in) round tin with shallow sides
(a pop-up base is handy but is not essential)

In Lydia Strangman's time they used to bunch up the violets at Kinoith and send them off to Covent Garden in London. When I started gardening at Kinoith I gathered up all the remnants of the violets I could find and made a violet bed. We do not know of a better way to remember Lydia than to crystallize the little flowers to use as precious decoration. We often make this delicious, rich little cake that keeps well in a tin for ages. A tiny slice is just perfect to nibble slowly with a demi-tasse of espresso or a cup of China tea. Violets appear early in spring and are over by May. The art of crystallizing flowers simply takes patience and a meticulous nature – the sort of job that drives some people around the bend but others adore. If it appeals to you, the work will be well rewarded – the violets look and taste divine. If properly done they will last for months. We store them in a pottery jar or in a tin box interleaved with kitchen paper.

Preheat the oven to 140°C/ 275°F/gas mark 1.

First crystallize the violets. The caster sugar ought to be absolutely dry, so for extra protection, sieve it and dry out on a Swiss roll tin in the preheated oven for about 30 minutes. Break up the egg white slightly with a fork – but it does not need to be fluffy. Using the clean paintbrush, brush the egg white very carefully and sparingly over each petal and into every crevice. Then gently sprinkle some caster sugar over the violet, coating every part thinly. Arrange the flower carefully on a baking parchment-lined tray and continue with the remaining violets. Leave to dry overnight in a warm dry place, such as an airing cupboard, close to a solid fuel cooker or over a radiator.

When you begin the cake, preheat the oven to 180°C/350°F/gas mark 4. Grease the tin well with melted butter and dust with a little flour. Put the ground almonds, icing sugar and flour into a bowl and mix thoroughly. Make a well in the centre and add the egg yolks and the cooled melted butter. Stir well until all the ingredients are thoroughly mixed. Spread the cake mixture evenly in the prepared tin, make a little hollow in the centre and tap on the work surface to release any large air bubbles.

Bake in the preheated oven for 40–45 minutes. The cake should still be moist but cooked through. Leave in the tin for 5–6 minutes before unmoulding on to a wire rack. Allow to cool.

Sieve the icing sugar into a bowl and mix to a thickish smooth icing with the boiling water. Use a palette knife, dipped in boiling water then dried, to spread the icing gently over the top and sides of the cake. Decorate with the crystallized violets and little diamonds of angelica.

Blackcurrant Leaf Lemonade

INGREDIENTS AS PAGE 46
750–900ml (1¹/₄ – 1¹/₂ pints) still or sparkling water
Ice cubes

Make as for Blackcurrant Leaf Sorbet (page 46) up to the point marked *, then add 750ml (1¹/₄ pints) of the water, taste and add more water if necessary. Serve chilled with lots of ice.

Summer

The garden bursts into life. After the lean months of spring suddenly there is an abundance of vegetables. It's impossible to use them all up but at last we're spoiled for choice! Broad beans come first and then we feast on one vegetable after the other: globe artichokes, baby carrots and tiny beetroot are pulled from the rich brown soil minutes before they're cooked and gobbled up; fresh and bright spinach, masses of rocket, radish, spring onion and all the good things of the salad bowl. Rampaging is all part of a logical whole as far as I'm concerned; we grow the stuff, we cook with it and the waste goes back to the hens, the compost, the pigs and so on.

The salad bowl is an integral part of lunch at the Cookery School. Up to 44 students come ravenously to the dining room, eager to taste the fruits of their labours during the morning. We use tiny ruby chard, carrot tops and mustard greens. Flowers too go into the tapestry – colourful chives, sage, nasturtiums and zucchini blossoms, and when we've plenty of these last we stuff them with local goat's cheese or tomato fondue.

Above: wild salmon smoked in the traditional way by Frank Hederman, one of the new breed of Irish artisanal food producers.

Right: choosing fresh lobsters for the School at Ballycotton.

Far right: looking out through the sound at Ballycotton. Our local fishermen are hard-working and courageous, landing their fresh catches whatever the weather.

The first of the smoked eel, warm from the smokehouse, signifies the start of summer. We feast on it, with a bit of lemon, soda bread and some of the very first vine-ripened tomatoes, grateful that Mrs Schwartau from Barnabrow had telephoned to tell us the eel was ready. Once the weather settles, out go the lobster pots. We have shrimps, crabs, summer plaice and lemon sole, which are sweet and tender and melting. The fishermen bring them into Ballycotton, the little fishing village on the coast two miles from us. Every Friday Dot Haynes drives over from Kilmacalogue Harbour on the Beara peninsula with whatever shellfish are in season, and we get scallops, palourdes, clams, sea urchins; sometimes she brings periwinkles and roghans (blue octopus), and from July onwards, she brings chanterelles and whatever other wild mushrooms she can find. Frank Hederman is the man from Belvelly who brings us mussels, salmon and eel, smoked in the old traditional ways. Bill Casey also smokes wonderful salmon on our farm too. The quality of fish we're offered is fantastic.

If we're lucky, new potatoes from the greenhouse coincide with the first salmon catch of the year, and the herb garden comes to a climax. It is based on a formal parterre, with little box hedges around each of the beds, in which we grow over 70 different herbs. We use the green leaves and flowers and later we dry some of the seeds like coriander, fennel and dill for spices. Fresh coriander goes into the Thai dishes we're experimenting with and into the salsas which we adore ever since our trip to Mexico.

The fruit garden is just outside the School's dining room. My friend Jim Reynolds, a great garden designer and plantsman, created the design for me and now it provides us with a fantastic crop of berries – loganberries, boysen-berries, Worcesterberries, yellow raspberries and the first strawberries which Timmy crushes to make muesli for us girls, Lydia, Emily and me, soaking a little oatmeal in water and sweetening it with some of our own honey and serving it for breakfast with rich cream and soft brown sugar. Delicious!

The Irish Peach tree has seven apples on the wall. It's an old apple variety I've rescued, so named because the fruit tastes of peaches. The almond tree is covered with soft, furry fruits for the first time. When Madhur Jaffrey was here

Above: Elizabeth O'Connell, my sister, is head gardener at Kinoith. She, Haulie and Eileen, front up the ace team which nurtures all our wonderfully abundant fresh produce.

Left: sunflowers (*Helianthus annus*) last incredibly well in flower arrangements; we harvest their edible seeds, and toast them to nibble, sprinkle over bread or add to winter salads.

Right: we are forever trying out new herbs, such as this one, ginger mint (*Mentha sauveolens* 'Variegta'), which makes a gorgeous flavouring for ice-cream.

Right: the beach hedges at Kinoith give tremendous shelter and also form marvellous architectural features, dividing the gardens and affording surprise views through their 'doorways'.

Far right: we grow many flowers at the Cookery School, some are for flavour, others for pleasure such as the many forms of *Lilium*. Nasturtium flowers decorate many fresh green salads beautifully. We also cultivate marguerites and petunias for summer colour.

Below: the herringbone paths of the vegetable garden form a diamond and are bisected by a cross. The bricks came from an architectural salvage yard.

she told us we could eat them whole when they're green. We've put the blueberries and cranberries in peat pots as they don't like our limey soil. It's difficult to believe that this garden is just five years old, the growth is truly amazing and the soil rich and fertile from all the farmyard manure, compost and seaweed that has been dug in. Our neighbours, the Walshes, three generations of them, have been growing more and more fruit – producing wonderful crops of tayberries, loganberries, boysenberries, raspberries, strawberries – to make into jams and jellies which we sell at the School. And Patty Walsh rears pigs too.

The barbecue course in mid-summer is the best fun. We teach the students about marinating and kebab-making, stretching their imaginations. We barbecue kidneys, fresh mackerel from the sea, butterfly legs of lamb and char-grill lots of vegetables. When I travel I might eat in some new restaurant or buy lots of cookbooks and that inspires me to try new dishes. Sometimes the recipe is exquisite exactly as it is and sometimes I wonder what it would taste like it if I add this or that to it. I write a few notes and try it. Not everybody's cookbooks delight me. Some I buy just for ideas but in others I follow every word of genius, like an apostle!

This year's garden development has been to plant the yew tree maze, which covers almost an acre. It was a nightmare to mark out – it couldn't be even a quarter of an inch out in the planting or it would look dreadful. It took ten days to plant; the design is based on an old Celtic pattern and was drawn out by my friend Peter Lamb. Lesley Beck reworked the design to ensure a strong puzzle and to provide a short exit. In ten to fifteen years' time it should have matured. Who'll trim the hedges? I've wanted to plant a maze since the Year of the Maze in 1992 and had the sudden brainwave of planting it as a present for Timmy. Amazingly he was not immediately thrilled by my gallant gesture, possibly suspecting that he might have to pay for it in the end. However, he came around, and now that it's finally planted, we're both thrilled with it. It's such a bit of nonsense and so kind of fantastically flamboyant, almost irresponsible. When I think of the money that has gone into it, but then I don't want a yacht in the Caribbean or anything like that. I prefer to put the money into creating gardens for all of us to enjoy throughout the seasons.

Spinach and Rosemary Soup

SERVES 6-8

55g (2oz) butter
115g (4oz) onion, chopped
140g (5oz) potatoes, chopped
Salt and freshly ground black pepper
225–350g (8–12oz) spinach,
destalked and chopped
600ml (1 pint) Home-made
Chicken Stock (see page 184), vegetable
stock or water
425–600ml (14fl oz–1 pint) creamy milk
(or use 1:3 cream:milk)
1 tablespoon chopped fresh rosemary

GARNISH
2 tablespoons whipped cream (optional)
Sprigs of rosemary

We have spinach all year round. You can use either perpetual or summer spinach. The trick with these green soups is not to add the greens until the last minute, otherwise they will overcook and you will lose the fresh taste and bright lively colour.

Melt the butter in a heavy-bottomed saucepan. When it foams, add the onions and potatoes and turn them until well coated. Sprinkle with salt and pepper. Cover and sweat on a gentle heat for 10 minutes. Add the boiling stock and milk, bring back to the boil and simmer until the potatoes and onions are fully cooked. Add the spinach and boil with the lid off for about 3–5 minutes, until the spinach is tender. Add the chopped rosemary. Liquidize, then taste. Serve in warm bowls garnished with a blob of whipped cream and a sprig of rosemary.

Pea and Coriander Soup

SERVES ABOUT 6

55g (2oz) butter
140g (5oz) onion, finely chopped
2 cloves garlic, peeled and chopped
1 green chilli, deseeded and
finely chopped
450g (1lb) fresh peas (good-quality
frozen ones are also fine)
900ml (1½ pints) Home-made Chicken
Stock (see page 184)
About 2 tablespoons freshly chopped
coriander
Salt and freshly ground black pepper
Sugar

GARNISH
Soflty whipped cream
Fresh coriander leaves

This utterly delicious soup has a perky zing with the addition of fresh chilli.

Melt the butter over a gentle heat and sweat the onion, garlic and chilli for 3–4 minutes. Add the peas and cover with the stock. Bring to the boil and simmer for 7–8 minutes. Add the freshly chopped coriander and liquidize in a blender. Season with salt and pepper and add a pinch of sugar, which enhances the flavour. Serve with a swirl of softly whipped cream and a few fresh coriander leaves.

Light Fish Soup with Spring Onions

SERVES 6

225g (8oz) lemon sole or plaice fillets, skinned

1.2 litres (2 pints) very well-flavoured Chinese Stock (see page 185)

Salt and lots of freshly ground white pepper

$\frac{1}{2}$ –1 red or green chilli, thinly sliced

18 prawns or 30 shrimps, cooked and peeled

1 generous iceberg lettuce heart, about 12 tablespoons, very finely shredded

GARNISH

6 teaspoons spring onions, finely sliced at an angle

Prawn or shrimp roe, if available

Fresh coriander or flat-leaf parsley

We adore these light fish soups. Consider this recipe as a formula and vary the fish and shellfish depending on what you have available – mussels and white crab meat are particularly delicious. We get Atlantic shrimps; if you are using the larger Pacific shrimp you will need fewer. Lemongrass and a dice of cucumber also work well.

Cut the fish fillets at an angle into pieces about 5cm (2in) wide. When you are ready to eat, bring the stock to the boil and add the salt, chilli and pieces of fish. Simmer for 1 minute. Add the prawns or shrimps and allow to heat through.

Put 2 tablespoons of the shredded lettuce into each soup bowl, season generously with pepper and immediately ladle the boiling soup over it. Garnish with spring onions, prawn or shrimp roe and lots of fresh coriander or flat-leaf parsley. Serve very hot.

Vine-ripened Tomato and Spearmint Soup

SERVES 6

1 onion – about 115g (4oz), finely chopped
15g (¹/₂oz) butter
750ml (1¹/₄ pints) Vine-ripened Tomato
Purée (see page 182)
230ml (8fl oz) Béchamel Sauce (see page
182)
230ml (8fl oz) Home-made Chicken
Stock (see page 184) or vegetable stock
About 2 tablespoons spearmint, freshly
chopped
Salt and freshly ground black pepper
Sugar

GARNISH

Whipped cream, with freshly chopped
spearmint leaves added

In late August we have a glut of intensely flavoured tomatoes and basil, which could also be used for this recipe. It is quite tricky to balance this soup – avoid making it too strong or too thick by diluting it with stock. It needs to be tasted carefully as the final result depends on the quality of the ingredients.

Sweat the onion in the butter on a gentle heat until soft but not coloured. Add the Vine-Ripened Tomato Purée, Béchamel Sauce and Home-made Chicken Stock. Add the chopped spearmint and season with salt, pepper and a good pinch of sugar. Bring to the boil and then simmer gently for a few minutes.

Liquidize, taste, and dilute further with stock if necessary. Bring back to the boil, correct the seasoning and serve with a swirl of the mint-flavoured cream.

Ballycotton Shrimps with Chilli, Coriander and Lemongrass

SERVES 8

CHILLI AND CORIANDER DRESSING
1/2 **fresh red chilli**
1/2 **stem lemongrass**
2 **tablespoons fresh coriander, coarsely chopped**
2¹/2 **tablespoons Nam pla (fish sauce – the Squid brand is a good one)**
3 **tablespoons freshly squeezed lemon juice**
2 **teaspoons soft brown sugar**
2¹/2 **tablespoons dry white wine**

450g (1lb) **fresh shrimps or Dublin Bay prawns, cooked and peeled**

GARNISH
Sprigs of fresh coriander

Many people are surprised to find lemongrass growing in Shanagarry but we have been growing it successfully in the greenhouse for the past year or so, and we have at last managed to divide and repot the original precious plants. At first I tended to use it sparingly but now, as it becomes ever more abundant, I have relaxed and use it lavishly to give many of our local foods a fresh and tangy Thai flavour. It works superbly with shrimps caught in Ballycotton Bay.

First make the dressing. Roll the chilli on the board to loosen the seeds and slice off the top. Taste a little – chillies vary a lot in degrees of heat, as you know! Shake out the seeds and chop all the flesh finely. Peel the outer leaves from the lemongrass and chop it finely too; then mix with the chilli, chopped coriander, fish sauce, freshly squeezed lemon juice, sugar and white wine in a bowl. Put the shrimps or prawns into the dressing, cover and leave to marinate in the refrigerator for 1–2 hours.

Serve the shellfish with some of the dressing spooned over the top. Garnish with sprigs of fresh coriander and serve with crusty bread.

Quesadillas with Squash Blossoms, Mozzarella, Guacamole and Tomato Salsa

SERVES 2-4

12–16 squash or 4–8 zucchini blossoms, depending on size
4 corn or wheat flour tortillas
225g (8oz) mozzarella (unless Oaxacan string cheese is available)
2 green chillies (optional)

GARNISH
Fresh coriander

ACCOMPANIMENTS
Guacamole (see page 187)
Tomato and Coriander Salsa (see page 187)

Quesadillas are one of the favourite snacks in Mexico. On Sundays in Oaxaca women make and sell these and many other delicious stuffed tortillas on little stalls in the streets and squares. Zucchini blossoms may also be used; they tend to be larger than squash flowers – one or at most two will be plenty for each quesadilla. A favourite filling for quesadillas in Oaxaca is simply grated Oaxacan string cheese (mozzarella is our nearest equivalent) and fresh squash blossoms.

First make the Guacamole and the Tomato and Coriander and Salsa, cover and keep cool. Remove the thorns from the base of the squash blossoms. Heat an iron pan or griddle; it should be medium hot, otherwise the outside of the tortillas will burn before the filling is cooked.

There are two ways of presenting quesadillas: one resembles a sandwich, the other a turnover. Lay a tortilla on the hot pan, put about 15g (¹/₂oz) of cheese on one half, keeping it a little from the edge, sprinkle some strips or dice of chilli on top with 3–4 squash blossoms or 1–2 larger zucchini blossoms and another 15g (¹/₂oz) of cheese. Fold the tortilla over the filling and cook for a minute or two, then turn over carefully. Cook just until the cheese begins to melt. Serve one or two per person with the Guacamole and the Tomato and Coriander Salsa.

Radishes with Butter, Crusty Bread and Sea Salt

Fresh radishes complete with leaves
Finest unsalted butter
Sea salt (we use Maldon flakes)

Crusty bread

When I was just nineteen, an au pair, alone and frightened in Besançon, a French girl took pity on me and invited me to have lunch with her in a café. We had a plate of charcuterie and radishes. I watched in fascination as she smeared a little unsalted butter on her radishes, dipped them in sea salt and ate them greedily. I followed suit – and I've never forgotten the flavour. We use Bill Hogan's fine unsalted butter churned from morning cream whenever we can get it.

Wash the radishes and trim the tail and the top of the leaves if they are long.

Cut a chunk of butter into 1cm (¹/₂in) cubes. If you have a pair of butter pats, soak them in cold water and then roll each cube into a ball, and drop then into a bowl of iced water.

To serve: put 7 or 8 chilled radishes on each plate, add 2 or 3 butter balls and a little mound of sea salt.

Serve fresh crusty bread as an accompaniment.

Stuffed Zucchini Blossoms with Goat's Cheese, Basil, Pesto and Tomato Fondue

SERVES 6–8

BATTER
140g (5oz) plain flour
1¹/₂ tablespoons olive oil
1–1¹/₂ free-range egg whites
Sea salt

Sunflower oil for deep-frying
12–16 zucchini flowers

FILLING
175–225g (6–8oz) fresh Irish goat's cheese (I use St Tola, Croghan or Ardsallagh, each wonderful but different)
3–4 teaspoons Pesto (see page 186)
3–4 tablespoons Tomato Fondue (see page 182)

ACCOMPANIMENT
Tomato sauce
or extra Tomato Fondue

In the summer we grow zucchini in both the kitchen garden and the greenhouses. They produce hundreds of canary yellow blossoms. The female flowers produce the fruit but we use the male flowers in our salads, as a container for sauces and in soups. They are also utterly delicious stuffed with a few melting morsels, then dipped in a light batter and deep-fried until crisp and golden. This may sound a fiddly recipe but it actually takes seconds. I only suggest this stuffing; let your imagination run riot. Any filling you choose should be juicy and melting.

First make the batter. Sieve the flour into a bowl and make a well in the centre. Pour in the olive oil, stir and add enough water to make a batter about the consistency of thick cream. Leave to stand for at least 1 hour if you can. Just before cooking, whisk the egg whites to a stiff peak and fold into the batter. Add salt to taste.

Heat the oil in a deep-fryer until very hot. Remove the thorns from the base of the zucchini flowers and the stamens from the centre. Hold a flower upright, open slightly and carefully. Put about 15g (¹/₂oz) goat's cheese, ¹/₂ teaspoon Pesto and 1 teaspoon Tomato Fondue into each. Twist the tip of the petals to seal. Dip in the batter and drop into the hot oil. Fry on one side for about 2 minutes and then turn over. They will take about 4 minutes in total to become crisp and golden. You may need to work in batches.

Drain on kitchen paper and serve immediately – just as they are or with hot tomato sauce or a little extra Tomato Fondue.

Char-grilled Summer Vegetables with Tapenade Toasts

SERVES 8 AS A STARTER (OR 4 AS A MAIN COURSE)

4 medium-sized green (or a mixture of green and golden) zucchini, sliced lengthways, 3mm ($1/8$ in) thick
2–3 aubergines, sliced, 5mm ($1/4$ in) thick
Sea salt
2–3 fleshy red peppers, Italian or Spanish if possible
2–3 fleshy yellow peppers, Italian or Spanish if possible
4–8 stalks of green asparagus
1 head of fennel, sliced lengthways, 3mm ($1/8$ in) thick
Salt and freshly ground black pepper
Extra virgin olive oil

Tapenade Toasts (see page 186)
Black olives

DRESSING
80ml ($2^3/4$fl oz) very best Italian extra virgin olive oil
Freshly squeezed juice of $1/4$ lemon or 2 tablespoons balsamic vinegar
10–12 whole basil leaves (annual marjoram is also very good)
Sea salt and freshly crushed black pepper (we crush ours in a pestle and mortar)

Whole Roast Garlic (see page 83)

In July we feast on these char-grilled vegetables as a starter. We use many different combinations. They are also marvellous with goat's cheese, with pasta and variously with Pesto.

Sprinkle the zucchini and aubergines with pure sea salt, leavethe slices to drain in a colander to get rid of the excess liquid – 30 minutes at least. However, if the zucchini are small, home-grown and very fresh, this step is scarcely necessary.

Char-grill the peppers, turning them so they become completely charred on all sides. We do this in various ways: on a char-grill, over the gas jet, under the grill or in the oven. Remove from the heat and place in a bowl. Cover and leave for 5–10 minutes. They will be easier to peel.

Blanch the asparagus in boiling salted water for no more than 30 seconds, then plunge into iced water to refresh. Drain.

Lay out the zucchini and aubergines on clean cloths or kitchen paper to dry off all the excess liquid. Brush each piece sparingly with olive oil. Grill the aubergines first using a char-grill or a hot grill pan – they should be soft when pressed and scorched by the grill but not blackened. Put each vegetable onto a large plate as it is cooked. Next char-grill or pan-grill the zucchini and fennel slices – just give them a few seconds to brown in the places where they touch the grill. Finally season the blanched asparagus stalks with salt and pepper. Grill for about $1/2$ minute on each side.

The peppers should now be cool. Peel off the charred skin and remove the stalk and seeds with your hands. Divide the peppers into four and add to the other char-grilled vegetables. Don't wash them or you will lose some of their sweet flavour.

Mix the extra virgin olive oil for the dressing with freshly squeezed lemon juice or balsamic vinegar.

Sppon the whisked dressing over the vegetables and toss gently. Taste and season with sea salt and freshly crushed black pepper. Arrange on a large platter and scatter with basil leaves, a few black olives and freshly cracked pepper and some sea salt.

Serve with Tapenade Toasts or bruschetta with a few Whole Roast Garlic.

Baked Plaice or Sole with Melted Butter and Summer Herbs

SERVES 4

4 very fresh plaice or sole on the bone
Salt and freshly ground black pepper
Water

HERB BUTTER
115g (4oz) butter
4 teaspoons finely chopped
mixed fresh parsley, chives, fennel and
thyme leaves

This delectable way of cooking fresh flat fish was the brainchild of my mother-in-law, Myrtle Allen. It can be used not only for plaice and sole but for all very fresh flat fish, such as brill, turbot, dabs, flounder and lemon sole. Depending on the size of the fish, it can be a starter or a main course. Because the fish is cooked on the bone with the skin on, it is particularly sweet and moist and may be eaten without sauce. Alternatively, it may be served not only with herb butter but with any other complementary sauce, such as Hollandaise, Beurre Blanc or Lobster. Make this dish from July to September, when plaice and sole are melting and tender, not during the winter when the flat fish are full of roe and out of season.

Preheat the oven to 180°C/350°F/gas mark 4.

Turn each fish on its side and remove the head. Wash the fish and clean the slits very thoroughly. With a sharp knife, cut through the skin right round the edge of each fish, just where the 'fringe' meets the flesh. Be careful to cut neatly and to cross the side cuts at the tail, or it will be difficult to remove the skin later on. Sprinkle the fish with salt and pepper and lay them in 5mm (¼in) of water in a shallow baking tin.

Bake in the preheated oven for 20–30 minutes according to the size of the fish. The water should have just evaporated as the fish is cooked. Check to see whether the fish is cooked by lifting the flesh from the bone at the head; it should lift off the bone easily and be quite white with no trace of pink.

Meanwhile, melt the butter, take off the heat and stir in the freshly chopped herbs. Just before serving, catch the skin down near the tail and pull it off gently (the skin will tear badly if not properly cut). Lift the fish on to hot plates and spoon the herb butter over them. Serve immediately with the remainder of the herb butter in a warm bowl.

To eat: first eat the flesh off the flat frame on top; then put your fork on top, slide your knife underneath the bone and flip it over gently on your plate. Lift back the underneath skin with your knife and continue to feast on the sweet flesh. Spoon a little more herb butter over if necessary.

Fresh Eel with Butter and Lemon

SERVES 4–6

900g (2lb) eel, skinned
Seasoned flour
25g (1oz) butter
1 lemon

GARNISH
Segments of lemon
Chopped parsley (optional)

As fresh fish is landed almost daily at Ballycotton we are unquestionably spoilt for choice. Yet if I were to be completely honest, my favourite fish of all is eel, a freshwater species. We so rarely get them, two or three times a year if we are lucky. I love them cooked in the simplest way just tossed in seasoned flour and cooked in butter. I have never had any desire to tart them up further. The fish will be so sweet and juicy that you will want to suck the bones – unthinkable but true!

Cut the eel into 7.5–10cm (3–4in) pieces and toss in seasoned flour. Melt the butter in a wide frying pan. Cook the pieces of eel over a medium heat, first on one side, then on the other, until just cooked through and golden. Transfer the fish to a serving dish or hot plates. Squeeze a little lemon juice into the butter in the pan, add a little more fresh butter if necessary and spoon the bubbling liquid over the fish. Serve immediately, maybe with a sprinkling of chopped parsley and some lemon segments.

Hot Buttered Lobster with Summer Herbs

SERVES 4

1.8 kg (4lb) live lobster; two weighing
900g (2lb) would be best
Salt

COURT BOUILLON
1 carrot
1 onion
600ml (1 pint) dry white wine
600ml (1 pint) water
Bouquet garni
5 or 6 black peppercorns

115g (4oz) butter
1–2 tablespoons of mixed herbs (flat-leaf
parsley, chives, thyme and fennel),
freshly chopped
Salt and freshly ground black pepper
Squeeze of lemon juice

GARNISH
Lemon segments
Fresh herbs

**VARIATION: HOT BUTTERED LOBSTER
WITH CHILLI AND CORIANDER**

1 red chilli, deseeded and chopped finely
1–2 tablespoons freshly chopped coriander

GARNISH
Lemon segments
Coriander leaves

One of the most exquisite ways to eat fresh lobster. In a perfect world the lobster should come straight from the sea, not a lobster tank. Lobster is becoming scarcer, so help to conserve the stocks by not buying a hen lobster, or undersized ones weighing less than a pound (about half a kilo).

Cook the lobsters by placing them in a pan with lukewarm salted water to cover. Use 115g (4oz) salt to every 2.4 litres (4 pints) water. Put the saucepan on a low heat and bring to simmering point slowly; lobsters expire at about 44°C (112°F). By this stage the lobsters will be changing colour, so remove them and discard all the cooking water.

Slice the carrot and onion for the court bouillon and put with the wine, fresh water, bouquet garni and peppercorns into a stainless-steel saucepan and bring to the boil. Replace the lobsters and cover with a tight-fitting lid. Steam the lobsters until they become bright red, then remove them from the pot. Strain the cooking liquid and reserve for a sauce.

As soon as the lobsters are cool enough to handle, split them in half, and extract all the meat from the body, tail and large and small claws. Scrape out all the soft, greenish tomalley (the liver) from that part of the shell nearest the head and put it with the firmer meat into a warm bowl wrapped in a tea towel.

Heat the lobster shells in a cool oven. Cut the lobster meat into chunks.* Melt half the butter and when it is foaming, add the lobster meat and the tomalley and toss until the meat is heated through and the juice turns pink, then add the summer herbs. Season with salt and pepper.

Spoon the lobster meat into the hot shells. Put the remaining butter into the pan to melt and scrape up any bits. Add a squeeze of lemon juice. Pour the buttery juices into small heated ramekins and serve alongside the lobster on hot plates. Garnish with sprigs of fresh herbs and lemon segments. Eat immediately.

Alternatively, try this delicious variation:

After you have heated the lobster shells, and cut the lobster meat into chunks,* melt half the butter and when it is foaming, add the chilli and cook for a minute. add the lobster meat and tomalley and toss. When the meat is heated through and the juice turns pink, add the coriander. Season with salt and pepper.

Roast Sea Bass with Roasted Cherry Tomatoes and Basil Oil

SERVES 6

18–24 red and yellow cherry tomatoes
Extra virgin olive oil
Salt and freshly ground white pepper
6 x 175g (6oz) fillets of sea bass, scaled
but not skinned
Basil Oil (see page 184)

GARNISH
Tiny basil leaves

Sadly sea bass has been overfished and is now becoming scarce. The skin, when it is crispy, is utterly delicious so don't leave it on your plate. Taste it and you will want to finish every morsel as well as the creamy flakes of tender fish underneath. Cod or hake fillets may be cooked in the same way.

Preheat the oven to 230°C/450°F/gas mark 8.

Toss the tomatoes in very little olive oil and season with salt and pepper. Roast in the preheated oven for 5–6 minutes or until they almost burst.

Meanwhile, score the fish quite deeply on the skin side to prevent it curling. Heat a thin film of olive oil in a non-stick pan to just below smoking point, then reduce the heat slightly.

Season the fillets and cook skin-side down in the pan until crisp and golden. Turn over on the other side and complete cooking in the preheated oven for a further 5–6 minutes depending on the thickness of the fillet. Alternatively, continue cooking on the stove if the fish fillet is more than 2.5cm (1in) thick.

Arrange skin-side up on a hot serving dish or individual plates. Pop a few oven-roasted red and yellow tomatoes around the edge. Drizzle with Basil Oil, garnish with tiny basil leaves and serve immediately.

Butterflied Leg of Lamb with Spices

SERVES 8–10

1 leg of lamb, weighing 2.2–2.6kg (5-6lb)

FOR THE MARINADE
2 teaspoons cumin seeds
1 teaspoon black peppercorns
1 teaspoon cardamom seeds
1 teaspoon chilli powder (optional)
1 teaspoon salt
5 tablespoons extra virgin olive oil
1 tablespoon balsamic or wine vinegar or sherry
3 garlic cloves, peeled and crushed

Although you can cook this dish indoors in the oven, it is also perfect for the barbecue and is a favourite on our summer barbecue course.

First, butterfly the leg of lamb: if it has already been boned, simply cut it open from top and bottom and lay it flat – it will roughly resemble the shape of a butterfly (hence the name). Otherwise, cut down along the leg and shank bone on the underside and carefully remove. Open out the lamb as above. You will need to make a few further cuts to allow the lamb to lie flat on the board.

Thick pieces of meat may be slightly opened out by slitting part of the way with a sharp knife. It is not necessary to get the meat all the same thickness – one of the attractions of this dish is that it provides a mixture of well-done and underdone pieces of meat. Remove any excess fat.

Roast the cumin seeds in a pan over a medium heat for 1-2 minutes and add the peppercorns and cardamom seeds. Remove from the heat and crush coarsely in a pestle and mortar. Mix the other marinade ingredients together in a bowl and add the ground spices. Put the lamb inside a large plastic bag and pour over the marinade; knot the end tightly. Leave in the fridge for 24 hours, turning from time to time.

Preheat the oven to 200°C/400°F/gas mark 6 and cook the lamb for 1–1½ hours, basting with marinade every 10 minutes. Rest the meat for 15-20 minutes before carving.

If you prefer to barbecue the lamb, light the barbecue and allow it to reach full heat. It's difficult to give a time for this, as barbecues vary so much.

Drain the lamb and arrange the rack at least 25cm (10in) from the coals – otherwise the inside will be raw while the outside is charred. It will take about 45 minutes to cook. During cooking, baste the lamb regularly with marinade. Rest the meat for 15-20 minutes before carving.

Serve with crusty potatoes, a good green salad and maybe apple and mint jelly or chutney.

Baby Beef Scallopini and Spinach with Raisins and Pine Kernels

SERVES 6

675g (1¹/₂lb) lean baby beef from the top round
Salt and freshly ground black pepper
Seasoned flour
Beaten free-range egg
Fresh white breadcrumbs
5–6 tablespoons clarified butter
Lemon segments

Spinach with Raisins and Pine Kernels
(see page 82)

We do not serve intensively reared veal either at Ballymaloe House or at the Cookery School but once or twice a year we have a naturally reared milk-fed calf from Sibylle Knobel or one of my own Kerry bull calves. The meat is not so pale as conventional veal but it is wonderfully sweet and delicious. This is one of Tim's favourite meals, reminding him of the Jersey baby beef of his childhood when his father was a Jersey breeder.

With a very sharp knife cut the top round into 5mm (¹/₄in) thick slices across the grain. Trim off any fat or sinews. Put between two sheets of plastic film and flatten a little more with a meat pounder or rolling pin. Dip each piece in well seasoned flour, beaten egg and soft white breadcrumbs. Pat off the excess.

Melt a little of the clarified butter in a wide frying pan. Fry the scallopini, a few at a time, until crisp and golden on one side, then flip over on to the other. Drain briefly on kitchen paper. Serve hot with segments of lemon and Spinach with Raisins and Pine Kernels.

Frittata with Oven-roasted Tomatoes and Summer Herbs

450g (1lb) cherry tomatoes
Salt and freshly ground black pepper
8 large eggs, preferably free-range
1 tablespoon freshly chopped parsley
2 teaspoons freshly chopped thyme leaves
1 tablespoon freshly chopped basil or marjoram
125g (4^1/$_2$oz) Gruyère cheese, freshly grated
40g (1^1/$_2$oz) Parmesan cheese, freshly grated
25g (1oz) butter
Extra virgin olive oil

YOU WILL NEED
non-stick frying pan with a 23cm (9in) top rim

ACCOMPANIMENT
Green salad leaves
Olives

Italian frittata , Middle Eastern kuku and Spanish tortilla all sound more exciting than a flat omelette, although that is basically what they are. Unlike their soft and creamy French cousin, these omelettes are cooked slowly over a very low heat – while you can be whipping up a delicious salad to accompany it! A frittata is cooked gently on both sides and served in wedges like a cake. Omit the tomato and you have the basic recipe, flavoured with cheese and a generous sprinkling of herbs. As with omelette, you will occasionally want to add some tasty morsels to ring the changes – perhaps spinach, ruby chard, calabrese, asparagus or smoked mackerel. The list is endless but be careful not to use the frittata as a dustbin – think about the combination of flavours before you empty your refrigerator!

Preheat the oven to 180°C/350°F/gas mark 4.

Halve the tomatoes around the equator and season with salt and a little pepper. Arrange in a single layer in a non-stick roasting tin and roast for 10–15 minutes, or until almost soft and slightly crinkly. Allow to cool.

Preheat the grill.

Whisk the eggs in a bowl. Add the salt, pepper, herbs, tomatoes and cheese to the eggs. Melt the butter in a non-stick frying pan. When the butter starts to foam, tip in the egg mixture. Lower the heat to its minimum. Use a heat-diffuser mat and gently cook the eggs for 15 minutes, or until the underneath is set. The top should still be slightly runny. Pop the pan under the pre-heated grill, about 4in (10cm) below the element, for 1 minute to set and barely brown the surface. Use a palette knife under the frittata to free it from the pan. Slide it on to a warm plate. Serve wedges with a green salad and a few olives, sprinkled with Parmesan and drizzled with the olive oil.

Pasta with Chanterelles, Tapenade and Flat-leaf Parsley

SERVES 4–6

4.5 litres (8 pints) water
1 tablespoon salt
225g (8oz) penne, conchiglie or farfalle
225–450g (8oz–1lb) chanterelles
30g (1oz) butter
Salt and freshly ground black pepper
120ml (4fl oz) cream
2–3 tablespoons Tapenade (see page 186)

GARNISH

2 tablespoons freshly chopped flat-leaf parsley

Dot Haynes, who delivers shellfish to the School, also brings chanterelles up to us from the Beara peninsula when they are in season (from late July to October).

Bring a large saucepan of water to a fast rolling boil, add the salt and the pasta. Stir and cook until *al dente*. Meanwhile, quickly but gently wash the chanterelles under cold running water. Trim the base of the stalks and discard. Slice the mushrooms thickly.

Melt the butter in a frying pan on a high heat. When it foams add the mushrooms. Season with salt and pepper. Cook on a high heat, letting the juices exude at first and then cook until the chanterelles re-absorb them. Add the cream and bubble for a minute or two. Stir in the Tapenade. Strain the pasta and drain well, put back into the saucepan, add the sauce. Sprinkle on the parsley, toss gently, turn into a hot bowl and serve immediately.

Summer Pasta with Zucchini and Sugar Snaps

SERVES 10

450g (1lb) green and golden zucchini,
13–15cm (5–6in) in length
450g (1lb) sugar snaps
Salt and freshly ground black pepper

450g (1lb) penne or spaghetti
55g (2oz) butter
4 tablespoons olive oil
2 tablespoons chopped parsley
55g (2oz) torn fresh basil leaves
175g (6oz) Parmesan cheese (Parmigiano
Reggiano is best), freshly grated

GARNISH
A few zucchini flowers, if available

Simple, yet – if the Parmesan is good and all the ingredients are fresh – a sublime dish.

Top and tail the zucchini and cut at an angle into 5mm (^{1}/4in) slices. String the sugar snaps if necessary. Bring 8 litres (12 pints) of water to the boil in a large deep saucepan and add 2 tablespoons salt. Add the pasta and cook until *al dente*. Meanwhile, shoot the sugar snaps into 1.2 litres (2 pints) of boiling water with 1^1/2 teaspoons of salt and cook, uncovered, for 3–4 minutes or until crisp and *al dente*, then drain. Pop a serving bowl for the pasta into the oven to warm or, better still, sit it on top of the pasta saucepan.

If you are adept at juggling and have enough stove space, you can fry the zucchini while the pasta and sugar snaps are cooking. Heat the butter and olive oil in a sauté pan, toss in the zucchini, increase the heat and continue to toss for 3–4 minutes. Season with salt and pepper, cover the pan and reduce the heat to medium for another few minutes, by which time the zucchini should be tender but still *al dente*; draw off the heat.

By now, if your timing is good, the pasta too should be *al dente*, so drain it quickly. Add the sugar snaps, chopped parsley and torn basil to the zucchini, pour in the steaming hot pasta, sprinkle on two-thirds of the freshly grated Parmesan and toss well. Taste and adjust the seasoning if necessary.

Turn into the hot serving bowl and garnish with a few zucchini flowers, if available, and basil leaves over the top. Rush to the table – serve on hot plates with the remaining Parmesan and freshly ground pepper.

Aigre-doux Onions with Thyme Leaves

SERVES 4–6

450g (1lb) button onions
25g (1oz) butter
2 teaspoons thyme leaves
25g (1oz) sugar
50ml (1¹/₂fl oz) vinegar or 2 tablespoons white wine vinegar
Salt and freshly ground black pepper

A basket of baby onions is a real treasure to have in the pantry; we save the small onions of the crop carefully – gorgeous for roasting, sweet and melting, cooked whole in stews or in onion Tartes Tatins and irresistible with a shiny sweet-sour glaze. Of course you can eat this dish all year round.

Peel and trim the onions, leaving the root base intact. Melt the butter in a heavy saucepan and toss the onions in it. Add the thyme leaves. Cover with a butter wrapper and a tight-fitting lid. Cook on a low heat until almost soft.

Add the sugar and vinegar, increase the heat and cook until the salt, vinegar and onion juices make a syrupy glaze. Spoon into a hot serving dish and serve immediately.

New Season Baby Broad Beans with Olive Oil and Orla Sheep's Milk Cheese

SERVES 6

New season broad beans – about 1.8kg (4lb) in the pods
Extra virgin olive oil
Sea salt
Orla sheep's cheese, Knockalara or Pecorino
Crusty white bread or ciabatta

As my 'garden angels', Eileen, Elizabeth and Haulie, know, broad beans, considered dull by many, are my favourite vegetable. I insist on planting the first seeds in November, so that with luck we will have the first tender beans in early June. With careful successive planting we still manage to have them until the end of October. I use the tangy-tasting, prize-winning sheep's cheese made by Ollie Jungwirth and Iris Diebrok from Manch Farm near Ballineen in West Cork because it is the perfect foil for broad beans – as is Knockalara sheep's milk cheese. Pecorino would be eaten in Italy; you could also use a feta or anything slightly crumbly and sharp.

Bring the broad beans to the table, have a bottle of your best extra virgin olive oil, a bowl of sea salt and a piece of sharpish sheep's milk cheese – we use Orla made from the milk of Friesland organic sheep raised on Manch Farm.

Let each person have the pleasure of removing the beans from the furry pods. When you have accumulated a little pile on your plate, dip them one by one, first into olive oil, then into sea salt. Enjoy with the tangy cheese and warm crusty bread or ciabatta. Thin slices of Parma ham (Prosciutto di Parma) or very good Italian salami would make a more substantial feast.

Okra in Batter

SERVES 4

225g (8oz) fresh okra (lady's fingers)
115g (4oz) plain flour
1¹/₂ tablespoons ground rice or rice flour
1 tablespoon cayenne pepper
¹/₂ teaspoon ground cumin
¹/₂ teaspoon ground turmeric
1 teaspoon salt
1 teaspoon thyme leaves
Olive oil for deep-frying

Among other exotics we grow okra in the greenhouses. Gumbos are quite a performance, delicious though they are, so try this simple recipe, to serve with fish or meat. We love to eat them with fishcakes.

Slice the caps off the okra and discard. Cut the stalks into 1cm (¹/₂in) thick rounds.

Sieve the plain flour, the ground rice or rice flour, cayenne pepper, cumin, turmeric and salt into a bowl. Add the thyme leaves, mix well and make a well in the centre. Add about 100ml (3¹/₂fl oz) water, and whisk in a little at a time, to make a light batter about the consistency of thick cream.

Heat the oil in a deep-fryer over a medium-low heat. Fold the slices of okra gently into the batter and drop tablespoonfuls into the oil carefully. Fry, turning now and then, until the fritters are crisp and golden. This will take about 6–7 minutes. Serve immediately. Okra may also be simply dipped in milk and seasoned flour and deep-fried until golden. Quite delicious!

Garden Herb and Herb Flower Salad with Basil Dressing and Parmesan Crisps

SERVES 4 AS A STARTER
OR SIDE SALAD

16 leaves of mixed lettuce and salad leaves – allow about 4 leaves per person

Sprigs of all or some of the following:
HERBS:
Mint, tarragon, dill, coriander, fennel, basil, marjoram, thyme, flat-leaf parsley, chives, red orach

FLOWERS:
Chive, nasturtium, marigold, coriander, zucchini

Parmesan Crisps (see page 188)

BASIL DRESSING
30ml (1fl oz) wine vinegar
80ml (3fl oz) Basil Oil (see page 184)
1/2 teaspoon mustard (Dijon or English)
1 small clove garlic, crushed
1 small spring onion
Sprig of parsley
Sprig of watercress
1/2 teaspoon salt
A pinch of sugar
A few grinds of black pepper

We have a huge wooden salad bowl in the School's dining room turned from Irish elm by Keith Mosse. It is used every singe day for as many as 50 people and is an important part of the School: the salad is different each day and the students are continually fascinated when they go out in the morning with one of the gardeners to pick for it. In summer it overflows with lettuces, edible flowers, herbs and little greens. We always list the contents on the blackboard – there can be up to 20 different ingredients. This more than anything seems to teach the students the potential of the garden. Many have forgotten the flavour of home-grown lettuce as most commercial salad leaves are grown hydroponically and have less taste.

Wash all the salad leaves and, if necessary, the herbs and flowers. Whizz all the ingredients for the dressing in a blender for a few seconds. Or you can mix the oil and vinegar in a bowl, then add the mustard, salt, pepper and mashed garlic. Finely chop the parsley, spring onion and watercress and add. Whisk before serving.

Next make the Parmesan Crisps.

Toss the leaves and herbs in just enough dressing to make them glisten and pile the salad on individual plates. Garnish with herb flowers and serve immediately with the Parmesan Crisps.

Right: box (*Buxus sempervirens*) outlines the pattern of the herb garden which was inspired by a visit to Villandry in the Loire valley.

Kinoith Summer Garden Salad

SERVES 4–6

A SELECTION OF:
butterhead lettuce, oakleaf lettuce, little gem, iceberg lettuce, saladisi, mysticana, lollo rosso, frisée, radicchio, red orach leaves, rocket (arugula), edible chrysanthemum leaves, wild sorrel leaves or buckler leaf sorrel, golden marjoram, salad burnet, borage or hyssop flowers, young nasturtium leaves and flowers, marigold petals, chive or wild garlic flowers, herb leaves, such as lemon balm, mint and flat-leaf parsley, green pea shoots, tiny ruby chard, spinach or beetroot leaves, zucchini blossoms or broad bean tips

HONEY AND HERB DRESSING
175ml (6fl oz) extra virgin olive oil
4 tablespoons cider vinegar
1 teaspoon Irish honey
1 clove garlic, crushed
2 tablespoons freshly chopped mixed herbs (parsley, chives, mint, watercress and thyme)
Salt and freshly ground black pepper

'Kinoith' is the name of our house and the location of the Cookery School. The name comes from the Celtic Ciún-áit *or* Cion-ait *which means 'quiet' or 'friendly place'. It has now been anglicized as there is no K in the Celtic alphabet.*

Wash and dry the lettuce and salad leaves. If large, tear into bite-sized bits. Put in a deep salad bowl, add the herb sprigs and edible flowers. Toss, cover and chill in a refrigerator for a few minutes.

To make the dressing, put all the ingredients into a screw-topped jar, adding salt and pepper to taste. Shake well to emulsify before use. Otherwise whizz all the ingredients in a food processor or liquidizer for a few seconds.

As a variation you could use 3 tablespoons of fresh lemon juice or wine vinegar instead of cider vinegar.

Just before serving, toss the salad in just enough dressing to make the leaves glisten – save the remainder of the dressing for another day.

Shanagarry Tomato Salad

One variety or a mixture of very ripe
vine-ripened tomatoes – try to include
some cherry tomatoes, pear-shaped
tomatoes and, if you can get them, the
pretty striped Green Zebra, which look
and taste particularly wonderful

Sea salt and freshly ground black pepper
Sugar
Extra virgin olive oil

Ballymaloe French Dressing
(see page 182) or
balsamic vinegar or white wine vinegar

GARNISH
Basil leaves or mint leaves

Tomatoes have been grown in the greenhouses here in Shanagarry since my father-in-law, Ivan Allen, built his first timber house in the winter of 1934. For years the crops were grown commercially but for the past eight to ten years we have concentrated on growing as many varieties as we have space for with total emphasis on flavour – yield is not a high priority and every tomato is ripened on the vine. Varieties we enjoy are Sweet 100, Green Zebra, Valencia and Golden Jubilee. We even grow the tiny Tumbler variety in hanging baskets interspersed with herbs outside the cottages and around the school. Freshly picked sweet-tasting tomatoes, piled high in baskets, are part of every day and tomato salads made from a mixture of colours, shapes and varieties are part of almost every menu in late summer and early autumn. Never store tomatoes in the refrigerator.

Cut the tomatoes in half or lengthways or into wedges or simply into 5mm (1/4in) thick slices depending on the shape and size. Spread out in a single layer on a large flat plate and season with sea salt, pepper and a little sugar. Sprinkle with Ballymaloe French Dressing or, sparingly, with balsamic vinegar and generously with extra virgin olive oil. Scatter with torn basil or mint leaves. Toss gently, just to coat the tomatoes. Serve soon either as a first course or as an accompanying salad.

Spinach with Raisins and Pine Kernels

SERVES 6

25–40g (1–1¹/₂oz) good seedless raisins
25–40g (1–1¹/₂oz) fresh pine kernels
1.3kg (3lb) fresh spinach
55g (2oz) butter
2 tablespoons extra virgin olive oil
Salt and freshly ground black pepper
A splash of balsamic vinegar

We grow perpetual spinach year round and annual spinach through the summer season. We use it in soups, salads, toppings for pizzas, as a vegetable, wilted, sautéed, puréed and sieved. It creates the green in pasta verde and the tiny succulent new leaves are a 'must have' in our summer green salads. For this recipe I prefer to use melting summer spinach but you could also use perpetual spinach with its slightly stronger flavour and more robust texture. It is particularly delicious with Baby Beef Scallopini (page 73) or Roast Pork with Crackling (page 120).

Put the raisins into a little bowl and cover them with boiling water for about 10 minutes so they become plump and juicy.

Meanwhile toast the pine kernels until they are golden brown. Remove the stalks from the spinach, wash in several changes of cold water and drain.

Cook in a large covered saucepan with no further liquid apart from that which adheres to the leaves after washing. Cook over a medium heat and toss once or twice. As soon as the leaves are tender, drain thoroughly and squeeze dry. Chop finely.

Melt the butter and oil in a sauté pan, add the spinach, raisins and pine kernels. Season well with salt and pepper. Allow to bubble for 4–5 minutes and add a splash of balsamic vinegar. Taste and correct the seasoning. Serve immediately.

Whole Roasted Garlic

SERVES 6–10
450g (1lb) whole garlic bulbs
600ml (1 pint) extra virgin olive oil
Salt and freshly ground black pepper
Sprig or two of thyme, rosemary
or sage (optional)

Save the left-over oil which will be deliciously flavoured with roast garlic for other dishes.

Preheat the oven to 180°C/350°F/gas mark 4.

Slice the top quarter off each head of garlic with a sharp knife. Arrange the garlic bulbs in a single layer in a shallow baking tray – we use a lasagne dish. Pour over the olive oil and season with salt and pepper. I sometimes tuck in a sprig or two of thyme, rosemary or sage. Cover with tin foil and bake for about an hour, by which time the garlic cloves will be beginning to pop out of their skins. Discard the foil and bake, uncovered, for a further 15–20 minutes or until golden brown.

Globe Artichoke Hearts Braised in Olive Oil

SERVES 4

900 ml (1¹/₂ pints) water
1 lemon
6 globe artichokes
1 onion, coarsely diced
6 tablespoons extra virgin olive oil
2 cloves garlic, chopped
4 tablespoons coarsely chopped parsley
Salt and freshly ground black pepper

Ireland has a great climate for globe artichokes. Fields of them make one of the more bizarre sights which greet tourists on the Beara peninsula. Our variety has been handed down through generations of Myrtle Allen's family. We mostly eat them whole, dripping with melted butter or Hollandaise. We grow so many that by the time August comes we get more flahulach *with them and just eat the hearts.*

Preparing the artichokes is the fiddliest part of this recipe. Acidulate the water with the juice of the lemon. Drop in the squeezed lemon halves too. Cut a ring around the stalk where it meets the base of the artichoke. Break off the stalk and the toughest fibres will come with it. Then, with a sharp knife, starting from the base, ruthlessly cut off all the leaves and trim the top down as far as the heart. Scrape out the hairy choke, either with the tip of a knife or a sharp-edged spoon. Work quickly and drop the trimmed hearts into the acidulated water immediately, or they will discolour.

Chop the onion into large dice. Heat the oil in a wide sauté pan, add the chopped onion and garlic and sweat for a few minutes. Cut the artichoke hearts into quarters or eighths, add to the pan with the chopped parsley. Season with salt and freshly ground pepper and toss well. Add 60ml (2¹/₂fl oz) water, cover and cook for 10–15 minutes, until the artichokes are tender. Serve hot or at room temperature.

Kohlrabi with Marjoram

SERVES 4–6

450g (1lb) kohlrabi
Butter
¹/₂–1 tablespoon annual marjoram
Salt and freshly ground white pepper

We grow both green- and purple-skinned kohlrabi; they are a wonderfully delicate vegetable and deserve to be better known. Use them while they are still young, not much bigger than a golf ball. Like turnips, they become woody as they get larger or if the summer is very dry.

Wash and peel the kohlrabi and slice it thickly. Melt the butter in a flame-proof casserole, toss the kohlrabi until it is barely coated. Season with salt and pepper. Add no more than a tablespoon of water and a sprig of annual marjoram. Cover with a butter wrapper or a piece of greaseproof paper and the lid of the casserole. Cook over a low heat for 8–10 minutes until the kohlrabi is just tender. Remove the cooked herbs and add a little freshly chopped herbs. Taste, correct the seasoning and serve. Watch the amount of marjoram so as not to overpower the delectable but delicate flavour of the vegetable.

Honey Lavender Ice-cream

SERVES 8–10

250ml (8¹/₂ fl oz) milk
450ml (³/₄ pint) cream
40 sprigs fresh lavender or less of dried
(use the blossom end only)
6 free-range egg yolks
175ml (6fl oz) pure Irish honey – we use
our own apple blossom honey, although
Provençal lavender honey would also
be wonderful

DECORATION
Sprigs of lavender

I make this richly scented ice-cream in June when the lavender flowers in the kitchen garden bloom. Lavender is at its most aromatic just before the flowers open. Serve it on its own on chilled plates and savour every mouthful.

Put the milk and cream into a heavy-bottomed saucepan with the lavender sprigs, bring slowly to the boil and leave to infuse for 15–20 minutes. This will both flavour and perfume the liquid deliciously. Whisk the egg yolks, add a little of the lavender-flavoured liquid and then mix the two together. Cook over a low heat until the mixture barely thickens and lightly coats the back of a spoon (be careful it does not curdle). Melt the honey gently – just to liquefy – and whisk into the custard. Strain out the lavender heads. Chill thoroughly and freeze, preferably in an ice-cream maker or sorbetière.

Serve decorated with sprigs of lavender.

Carrageen Moss Pudding with Crushed Blueberries

SERVES 4–6

8g (¹/₄oz) cleaned, well dried
carrageen moss (1 semi-closed fistful)
850ml (28fl oz) milk
¹/₂ teaspoon pure vanilla essence or a
vanilla pod
1 egg, preferably free-range
1 tablespoon caster sugar
Blueberries or, better still, wild bilberries
or *fraughans*
Caster sugar
Softly whipped cream
Soft brown (Barbados) sugar

Carrageen moss is bursting with goodness. I ate it as a child but never liked it as it was always too stiff and unpalatable. Myrtle Allen changed my opinion! Hers was always so light and fluffy. I even had it for our wedding feast, made with fraughans (bilberries). Alas, the dye from the fraughans dyed all the guests' gums purple, to the consternation of our photographer.

Soak the carrageen in tepid water for 10 minutes. Strain off the water and put the carrageen into a saucepan with the milk and vanilla pod, if used. Bring to the boil and simmer very gently with the lid on for 20 minutes. At that point and not before separate the egg, put the yolk into a bowl, add the sugar and vanilla essence and whisk together for a few seconds; then pour the milk and carrageen moss through a strainer on to the egg yolk mixture, whisking all the time. The carrageen will now be swollen and exuding jelly. Rub all this jelly through the strainer and beat it into the flavoured milk. Test for a set in a saucer as one would gelatine. If it is a little soft, add back a little milk and push more carrageen through the sieve.

Whisk the egg white stiffly and fold it in gently with a whisk. It will rise to make a fluffy top. Leave to cool, then chill until set. Just before serving, crush the blueberries slightly with a potato masher, sprinkle generously with caster sugar and mix well. Serve the carrageen with the berries and cream and a sprinkle of soft brown sugar for a divine combination of flavours.

Summer Berries with Sweet Geranium Leaves

SERVES 8–10

100g (3¹/₂oz) raspberries
100g (3¹/₂oz) loganberries
100g (3¹/₂oz) redcurrants
100g (3¹/₂oz) blackcurrants
100g (3¹/₂oz) strawberries
100g (3¹/₂oz) blueberries
75g (2¹/₂oz) fraises des bois (wild strawberries – optional)

SYRUP
400g (14oz) sugar
450ml (³/₄ pint) water
6–8 large sweet geranium leaves

DECORATION
Sweet geranium leaves

Sweet geranium (Pelargonium graveolens) *and many other varieties of scented geraniums are ever present on our windowsills here at Ballymaloe. We use the delicious lemon-scented leaves in all sorts of ways. Occasionally, we also use the pretty purple flowers to enliven and add magic to otherwise simple dishes. The leaves can be crystallized and are wonderful with fresh cream cheese and fat juicy blackberries. I discovered this recipe, which has now become a perennial favourite, quite by accident a few summers ago as I raced to make a pudding in a hurry with the ingredients I had at that moment.*

Put all the freshly picked berries into a serving bowl. Put the sugar, cold water and sweet geranium leaves into a stainless-steel saucepan and bring slowly to the bowl, stirring until the sugar dissolves. Boil for just 2 minutes. Then pour the boiling syrup over the fruit and leave to macerate for several hours. Remove the geranium leaves. Serve chilled, with softly whipped cream, Ballymaloe Vanilla Ice-cream (see page 173) or on its own. Decorate with a few fresh sweet geranium leaves.

Honey Lavender Ice-cream

250ml (8¹/₂ fl oz) milk
450ml (³/₄ pint) cream
40 sprigs fresh lavender or less of dried
(use the blossom end only)
6 free-range egg yolks
175ml (6fl oz) pure Irish honey – we use
our own apple blossom honey, although
Provençal lavender honey would also
be wonderful

DECORATION
Sprigs of lavender

I make this richly scented ice-cream in June when the lavender flowers in the kitchen garden bloom. Lavender is at its most aromatic just before the flowers open. Serve it on its own on chilled plates and savour every mouthful.

Put the milk and cream into a heavy-bottomed saucepan with the lavender sprigs, bring slowly to the boil and leave to infuse for 15–20 minutes. This will both flavour and perfume the liquid deliciously. Whisk the egg yolks, add a little of the lavender-flavoured liquid and then mix the two together. Cook over a low heat until the mixture barely thickens and lightly coats the back of a spoon (be careful it does not curdle). Melt the honey gently – just to liquefy – and whisk into the custard. Strain out the lavender heads. Chill thoroughly and freeze, preferably in an ice-cream maker or sorbetière.

Serve decorated with sprigs of lavender.

Carrageen Moss Pudding with Crushed Blueberries

SERVES 4–6

8g (¹/₄oz) cleaned, well dried
carrageen moss (1 semi-closed fistful)
850ml (28fl oz) milk
¹/₂ teaspoon pure vanilla essence or a
vanilla pod
1 egg, preferably free-range
1 tablespoon caster sugar
Blueberries or, better still, wild bilberries
or *fraughans*
Caster sugar
Softly whipped cream
Soft brown (Barbados) sugar

Carrageen moss is bursting with goodness. I ate it as a child but never liked it as it was always too stiff and unpalatable. Myrtle Allen changed my opinion! Hers was always so light and fluffy. I even had it for our wedding feast, made with fraughans (bilberries). Alas, the dye from the fraughans dyed all the guests' gums purple, to the consternation of our photographer.

Soak the carrageen in tepid water for 10 minutes. Strain off the water and put the carrageen into a saucepan with the milk and vanilla pod, if used. Bring to the boil and simmer very gently with the lid on for 20 minutes. At that point and not before separate the egg, put the yolk into a bowl, add the sugar and vanilla essence and whisk together for a few seconds; then pour the milk and carrageen moss through a strainer on to the egg yolk mixture, whisking all the time. The carrageen will now be swollen and exuding jelly. Rub all this jelly through the strainer and beat it into the flavoured milk. Test for a set in a saucer as one would gelatine. If it is a little soft, add back a little milk and push more carrageen through the sieve.

Whisk the egg white stiffly and fold it in gently with a whisk. It will rise to make a fluffy top. Leave to cool, then chill until set. Just before serving, crush the blueberries slightly with a potato masher, sprinkle generously with caster sugar and mix well. Serve the carrageen with the berries and cream and a sprinkle of soft brown sugar for a divine combination of flavours.

Fresh Apricot Tart

SERVES 10–12

PASTRY
225g (8oz) plain flour
175g (6oz) butter
Pinch of salt
2 teaspoons icing sugar
A little beaten free-range egg or egg yolk and water to bind

APRICOT GLAZE
6 tablespoons apricot jam
Freshly squeezed lemon juice

FILLING
8–10 fresh apricots
2 large or 3 small eggs
2 tablespoons caster sugar
1 teaspoon pure vanilla essence
300ml (1/2 pint) cream

YOU WILL NEED
1 x 30cm (12in) diameter tart tin or
2 x 18cm (7in) diameter tart tins with removable bases

This is my version of a tart I first tasted when I was a rather reluctant au pair in France many years ago; it is now one of our favourites. Apples, pears, gooseberries, rhubarb and plums are also good and the custard could be flavoured with a little cinnamon instead of vanilla if you want to ring the changes.

Preheat the oven to 180°C/350°F/gas mark 4.

Make the shortcrust pastry in the usual way (see page 183) and leave to relax in a refrigerator for 1 hour. Roll out the pastry and line a tart tin (or tins) with a removable base and chill for 10 minutes. Line with kitchen paper and fill with dried beans. Bake blind in a preheated oven for 15–20 minutes. Remove the paper and beans. Paint the tart base with a little egg wash and return to the oven for 3–4 minutes. Leave to cool.

In a small stainless-steel saucepan, melt the apricot jam with a squeeze of lemon juice, push the hot jam through a sieve and then brush the base of the tart with a little of the glaze.

Halve the apricots and remove the stones. Arrange one at a time cut-side upwards inside the tart; the apricots should slightly overlap in the inside.

Whisk the eggs well with the sugar and vanilla essence, then add the cream. Pour this mixture over the apricots and bake in the preheated oven for 35 minutes. When the custard is set and the apricots are fully cooked, brush generously with the apricot glaze and serve warm with a bowl of softly whipped cream.

Peach and Raspberry Crisp

SERVES ABOUT 8

115g (4oz) plain white flour
230g (8oz) brown sugar
340g (12oz) organic oat flakes
1/4 teaspoon freshly ground nutmeg
1/3 teaspoon cinnamon, ground
225g (8oz) butter, melted

900g (2lb) peaches or nectarines
340g (12oz) raspberries
1 tablespoon cornflour

YOU WILL NEED

Lasagne-type dish approx 30 x 25cm
(12 x 10in)

In the summer of 1996 I spent a few days at Zingermann's deli in Ann Arbor in Michigan, where they make sensational sandwiches, salads and puddings. Ari Weinzweig sent me the recipe for this delicious pudding.

Preheat the oven to 180°C/350°F/gas mark 4.

Put all the dry ingredients into a bowl, add the melted butter and mix until crumbly. Slice the fruit into the ovenproof dish. Sprinkle with the cornflour and mix well. If the fruit is unusually tart you may need a little sugar. Top with a generous and even layer of crumble mixture. I use about 450g (1lb) and keep the rest for another day to use with plums or greengages.

Bake the dish in the preheated oven for 30–40 minutes or until the topping is crisp and the fruit tender. The juices should bubble up through the edges. Serve with softly whipped cream.

Lemon Verbena and Lemon Balm Sorbet

SERVES ABOUT 8

225g (8oz) sugar
600ml (1 pint) cold water
2 large handfuls of lemon verbena and
lemon balm leaves
Freshly squeezed juice of 3 lemons
1 free-range egg white (optional)

DECORATION

Lemon verbena and lemon balm leaves

Rory O'Connell, my brother, serves this deliciously fresh sorbet as a starter at Ballymaloe House; it just flits across the tongue and scarcely needs to be swallowed. A perfect start to a late summer meal.

If you don't have a sorbetière, simply freeze the sorbet in a bowl in the freezer. When it is semi-frozen, whisk until smooth and return to the freezer again. Whisk again when almost fully frozen and fold in one stiffly beaten egg white. Keep in the freezer until needed. If you have access to a food processor, simply freeze the sorbet completely in a baking tray, then break up and whizz for a few seconds in the processor. Drop one slightly beaten egg white down the tube, whizz again and freeze. Serve as below.

Put the first three ingredients into a non-reactive saucepan and bring to the boil slowly; simmer for 2–3 minutes. Then leave to get quite cold. Add the lemon juice. Strain and freeze for 20–25 minutes in an ice-cream maker or sorbetière. Serve in chilled glasses or chilled china bowls. Decorate with lemon verbena and lemon balm leaves.

Meringue Roulade with Summer Strawberries and Fresh Raspberry Sauce

SERVES 6

4 free-range egg whites
225g (8oz) caster sugar
300ml (¹/₂ pint) whipped cream
350–450g (12–16oz) fresh strawberries

DECORATION
6 whole strawberries
Free-range egg white
Caster sugar
Sprigs of mint, lemon balm or sweet cicely

FRESH RASPBERRY SAUCE
6–8 tablespoons Sugar Syrup (see page 93)
225g (8oz) raspberries
Lemon juice (optional)

YOU WILL NEED
Swiss roll tin 30 x 20cm (12 x 8in)

This roulade is also very good filled with raspberries, loganberries, sliced peaches, nectarines, kiwi fruit – even sliced bananas tossed in lemon juice.

Preheat the oven to 180°C/350°F/gas mark 4.

Put the egg whites into the spotlessly clean bowl of a food mixer. Break up with the whisk and then add all the caster sugar in one go. Whisk at full speed until it holds a stiff peak, about 4–5 minutes.

Meanwhile, line a Swiss roll tin with tin foil and brush lightly with a non-scented oil, such as sunflower or groundnut. Spread the meringue gently over the tin with a palette knife – it should be quite thick and bouncy.

Bake in the preheated oven for 15–20 minutes. Put a sheet of tin foil on the work top and turn the roulade on to it. Remove the base tin foil carefully and leave the meringue to cool.

Liquidize the raspberries with the syrup and sieve, then taste and sharpen with lemon juice if necessary. Store in the refrigerator.

To assemble, spread the whipped cream over the roulade. Slice the strawberries and mix with a little of the Raspberry Sauce. Spread the fruit and the cream on the meringue. Roll up from the narrow end and ease carefully on to a serving plate.

Dip the remaining strawberries in a very little egg white and sprinkle with caster sugar. Pipe six rosettes of whipped cream along the top of the roulade. Decorate with the sugared strawberries or just fresh strawberries and mint leaves.

Serve cut into slices about 2.5cm (1in) thick, accompanied by a little fresh Raspberry Sauce.

Loganberry Tart or Tartlets

SERVES 12

115g (4oz) butter
115g (4oz) caster sugar
115g (4oz) ground almonds (use the best you can afford)
4–6 tablespoons of redcurrant jelly
450g (1lb) loganberries (or use raspberries, poached rhubarb, sliced peaches or nectarines, pipped and peeled grapes or kiwi fruit)

DECORATION
Lemon balm or sweet geranium leaves

330ml (10fl oz) whipped cream

YOU WILL NEED
2 x 18cm (7in) sandwich tins or a 24 patty tin

This crisp almond tart base takes just minutes to make and is particularly delicious with tangy berries or carefully poached rhubarb.

Preheat the oven to 180°C/350°F/gas mark 4.

Cream the butter and the caster sugar, add the ground almonds and mix just long enough to bring the ingredients together. Divide the mixture between the sandwich tins or put a teaspoon of mixture into each of the patty tin hollows. Bake in the preheated oven for about 20–30 minutes or until golden brown.

The tarts or tartlets will be too soft to turn out immediately, so cool for about 5 minutes before removing from the tins. Do not allow them to set hard or the butter will solidify and they will stick to the tins. if this happens, pop the tins back into the oven for a few minutes so the butter melts and then they will come out easily. Allow to cool on a wire rack.

Just before serving, arrange the whole loganberries on the base and glaze with redcurrant jelly. Pipe a little whipped cream around the edge and decorate with lemon balm or sweet geranium leaves.

Fraises des Bois Ice-cream with Strawberry and Rhubarb Compote

Rhubarb and strawberries marry wonderfully and now that strawberries have a longer season, we can enjoy them together. The secret to cooking rhubarb for a compote is to let it boil for just 1 minute in the hot syrup. Unlike plums, gooseberries or apricots the fruit must keep its shape. It is fabulous for breakfast. Serve it icy cold.

First make the ice-cream. Dissolve the sugar in the water, boil for 7–10 minutes, then leave to cool. Purée the strawberries in a food processor or blender and sieve. Add the orange and lemon juice to the cold syrup. Stir into the purée, then fold in the whipped cream. Freeze immediately in a sorbetière or ice-cream maker according to the manufacturers' instructions.

SERVES 6

FRAISES DES BOIS ICE-CREAM
225g (8oz) caster sugar
300ml (10fl oz) water
900g (2lb) very ripe wild strawberries
Juice of $\frac{1}{2}$ orange
Juice of $\frac{1}{2}$ lemon
150ml ($\frac{1}{4}$ pint) whipped cream

STRAWBERRY AND RHUBARB COMPOTE
450g (1lb) red rhubarb, such as Timperley Early

450ml ($\frac{3}{4}$ pint) Stock Syrup (see below)

225–450g (8oz–1lb) fresh strawberries, such as Cambridge Favourite, Elsanta or Rapella

DECORATION
Mint leaves or lemon balm leaves

STOCK SYRUP
450g (1lb) sugar
600ml (1 pint) water
Dissolve the sugar in the water and bring to the boil. Boil for 2 minutes, then leave it to cool. Store in the refrigerator until needed.

Next make the compote. Cut the rhubarb into 2.5cm (1in) pieces. Put the cold syrup into a stainless-steel saucepan and add the rhubarb. Cover the pan, bring to the boil and simmer for just 1 minute, then turn off the heat and leave the rhubarb in the covered saucepan until just cold. The fruit will be tender and plump. Hull the strawberries and leave them whole or slice lengthways, then add them to the rhubarb compote.

To serve: scoop out the ice-cream into a pretty glass bowl and serve with the chilled compote. Decorate with fresh mint or lemon balm leaves.

Home-made Cottage Cheese with Fresh Herbs and Crackers

MAKES ABOUT 450G (1LB) CHEESE

2.4 litres (4 pints) full-cream milk
1/2 teaspoon liquid rennet (you can get vegetarian rennet too)

YOU WILL NEED
Good-quality muslin or cheesecloth

HOME-MADE CRACKERS
MAKES 25-30

115g (4oz) brown wholemeal flour
115g (4oz) white flour, preferably unbleached
1/2 teaspoon salt
1/2 teaspoon baking powder
25g (1oz) butter
5-6 tablespoons cream

2-4 tablespoons freshly chopped herbs (parsley, chives, chervil, lemon balm and perhaps a little tarragon and thyme)
2-3 cloves garlic, crushed (optional)
Salt and freshly ground black pepper

This is super-easy to make and people are bowled over with admiration when you produce home-made cheese and crackers.

Put the milk into a spotlessly clean stainless-steel saucepan. Heat it very gently until it reaches the shivery stage and is barely tepid. Add the rennet, stirring it well into the milk.

Cover the saucepan with a clean tea towel and the lid. (The tea towel prevents the steam from condensing on the lid of the pan and falling back on to the curd.) Set aside and leave undisturbed somewhere in your kitchen for 2–4 hours, by which time the milk should have coagulated and will be solid.

Cut the curd into dice with a spotlessly clean knife. Put back on a very low heat and warm gently until the whey starts to run out of the curds. It must not get hot or the curd will tighten and toughen too much. Ladle into a muslin-lined colander over a bowl. Tie the corners of the cloth together and leave to drip overnight.

To make the crackers: preheat the oven to 180°C/350°F/gas mark 4.

Mix the brown and white flours together and add the salt and baking powder. Rub in the butter and moisten with enough cream to make a firm dough. Roll out very thinly – about 1.5mm (1/16in) thick. Prick with a fork and cut into 6cm (2 1/2in) squares, diamonds or rounds. Bake in the pre-heated oven for 20–25 minutes or until lightly browned and quite crisp. Cool on a wire rack.

Sieve the cottage cheese. Mix in the freshly chopped herbs and garlic if using. Season to taste. It may even need a pinch of sugar. Transfer the cheese to a pretty bowl and serve with home-made crackers.

Lemongrass Lemonade

MAKES ABOUT 2 PINTS

SYRUP
600ml (1 pint) water
450g (1lb) sugar
2 stems lemongrass, finely sliced

FOR THE LEMONADE
3 lemons
300ml (8fl oz) lemongrass syrup
950ml (32fl oz) water

If you live in a rural area, or indeed far from a good greengrocer, and you want to have access to exotic ingredients the only solution is to grow your own. That is what we did with lemongrass and now we have so much that we can afford to use it liberally in all sorts of ways, for instance in this refreshing and delicious drink.

First make the syrup. Put the cold water and sugar into a saucepan with the finely sliced lemongrass. Bring the mixture slowly to the boil and simmer for 2 minutes. Allow it to cool. Strain out the lemongrass.

When the syrup is cold, juice the lemons and mix the freshly squeezed juice with the water and 8 fl oz of lemongrass syrup in a jug. Keep the remainder in the fridge for another day. Mix well, taste and dilute with more water if necessary.

Serve chilled.

Tisanes

Water
Fresh herbs (such as lemon verbena, rosemary, sweet geranium, lemon balm, spearmint or peppermint)

We make lots of fresh herb infusions. If you have fresh herbs available, all you need to do is pop a few leaves into a teapot and pour on the boiling water – infinitely more delicious. I have a particular aversion to the little tea bags that are frequently used.

I am very wary about ordering herb tea in a restaurant for this reason but one Paris restaurant where I dined recently served herb infusions in the most delightful way. The waiter came to the table with several china bowls of fresh herbs on a silver salver. With tiny tongs he put the guests' chosen herb into a little china teapot, poured on boiling water and served it with a flourish. Exquisite.

Bring fresh cold water to the boil. Scald a china teapot, take a handful of fresh herb leaves and crush them gently in your hand. The quantity will depend on the strength of the herb and how intense an infusion you enjoy. Put them into the scalded teapot. Pour the boiling water over the leaves, cover the teapot and leave to infuse for 3–4 minutes. Serve immediately in china cups.

$\mathcal{A}$utumn

As soon as the September students settle in, I take them foraging and autumn is the best time. They think I'm crazy but I tell them how foraging is all the rage on the West Coast of America. 'Chez Panisse' in Berkeley has its own forager as has the Herb Farm in Seattle and Sooke Harbour House on Vancouver Island. We go along the hedgerows into the fields and on to the beach where we find a multitude of things like damsons, sloes, blueberries, blackberries, seaweeds, samphire, sorrel, wild mushrooms, periwinkles and mussels. They learn to make blackberry jam and damson jam, we make crab-apple jelly with sweet geranium leaves, rich elderberry jelly. We make sorrel soup and are probably the only people in the area who collect seaweed from the strand (beach); years ago there were pitched battles over the seaweed, before artificial fertilizers became widely available.

We introduce the students to the gardens and the gardeners who grow the produce they will cook. I talk to them about growing organically. If I had it my way all the surrounding farmland beyond our 100 acres would be organic too. We use no artificial fertilizers; just compost, manure, peat moss and seaweed. Elizabeth O'Connell, Haulie Walsh and Eileen O'Donovan, look after the gardens. The vegetable garden was laid out painstakingly, with old brick herringbone paths, by Frank Walsh in 1989 and it is now a formal pattern, a diamond bisected by a cross, filled with a delicious and hugely varied array of vegetables, such a treat to harvest in the early autumn. It is designed to be decorative as well as functional. But what happens now that everything is planted in patterns? Sometimes I can scarcely bear to cut a lettuce for fear of ruining the symmetry! In the garden we seem to be able to grow pretty much anything we want – grapes, almonds, Asian pears, olives, figs, nectarines, as well as mulberries, cranberries and blueberries. We've also grown chillies successfully outside, and oriental vegetables: pak choi, mibuna, mustard greens and garland chrysanthemum leaves. In the greenhouses, there's still lots of lemongrass and many different varieties of tomatoes, cucumbers, and all sorts of beans.

Ollie and Iris from Manch Farm supply us with organic sheep's milk ricotta, Orla cheese and thick, delicious yoghurt. Ina Korner brings goat's milk yoghurt and cheese from near Youghal; all the people work like mad to produce these exquisite foods; we are fortunate to have a network of fantastic suppliers and the whole locality can benefit from their brilliance. I feel so deeply grateful to all artisanal producers. We must all support them to help them flourish.

Left: behind the house and gardens at Kinoith is pastureland, grazed by our Kerry cows.

Right: we grow teazels (*Dipsacus fullonum*) for later winter flower decorations.

On the three-month courses, the students meet the gardeners each morning on a rota basis to pick the herbs and fruit and vegetables; on the short courses, that's an option if they are very keen. This is certainly one of the things that makes this cookery school pretty much unique for many people. It's also something that our guest chefs greatly enjoy. Many of my culinary idols have taught here: Madhur Jaffrey, Claudia Roden, Jane Grigson, Marcella Hazan, Sri Owen.

My culinary influences come from so many different people. I think immediately of the late Elizabeth David – so many of her recipes are completely delicious and still retain their currency even when times change. Julia Child too is a great influence. I learned much from my mother, Elizabeth O'Connell, whose cooking I took totally for granted as a child. Then of course Myrtle Allen, my mother-in-law, has always been, and continues to be, a huge inspiration; I find her to be a visionary, yet overwhelmingly modest. She has a tremendous confidence which allows her to cook as she wants with no regard for the latest fleeting fashion.

Below: the fruit garden may give the Cookery School students their first real opportunity to pick fruit straight from the trees and we try to make them aware of the abundance of wild food and the excitement of foraging.

Above: a corner of the vegetable garden. The tones of the beach hedge in autumn blend well with those of the Whichford pots which are used to blanch sea kale. The marvellous ironwork around the School is made by our blacksmith extraordinaire, Andy Grierson.

I've been collecting old roses for several years, Richard Wood has given me many and they've been sitting around in tubs while I plan my rose garden which I hope will eventually be in the old orchard. I also have plans for an Irish Garden with an emblem for each of the four provinces - the red hand of Ulster, the harp of Leinster, the three crowns for Munster and the eagle and sword for Connaught. I adore eighteenth-century gardens and long to do a double beech circle with a pond in the centre like the one I saw at Kilruddery outside Dublin, such beautiful gardens. And I want to plant the Irish Apple Collection: there

Above: Chervil and Rocket (our donkeys) were a present from the students of one of 1996's three-month courses.

Left: the 'Palais de Poulets' is home to our extensive collection of hens. Frank and JP collect their eggs which we then use in the School. These eggs have, for many people, a forgotten flavour.

Right: all our pigs lead a happy life which leads, in the end, to sweeter pork.

would certainly be over a hundred, maybe more. Always plans! I feel terribly fortunate that we inherited Kinoith, even though the gardens were a wilderness for a time. If someone hadn't planted them back in the 1830s I would never have had a base to restore and build on, so I am giving back to a certain extent by planting for the next generation. I hope that the gardens catch my children's imagination; it would be great if they could give even one member of the family tremendous pleasure.

I saw a herd of Kerry cows when travelling around Ireland with my TV crew filming for Irish television, so I bought an in-calf heifer from an organic farmer, Ivan Ward, who has since become a friend and advisor. (Eileen, who is one of my garden angels and a farmer's daughter from West Cork, had the misfortune to say she could milk a cow. Haulie, who helps us in the gardens, holds the cow at one end and Eileen milks it at the other.) In the autumn, the cows appear to shake the apple trees in the orchard while the pigs stand underneath munching the apples that fall. I was so disenchanted with the quality of pork that I bought a couple of saddleback sows. They needed a mate so I bought this Berkshire boar from a man I met up walking in the Comeragh mountains, so Black Pudding, as he is called, is the daddy and then we had Rasher and Sausage. Sausage went off to be made into sausages. We've had lots and lots of litters since then and they are all happy, lazy pigs – unlike the majority of pigs, which are reared in intensive units and have nothing in the world to recommend them and their meat has no flavour. We don't feel that we have the right to keep animals unless they are comfortable and are kept in humane conditions. I feel that very, very strongly and, though I have no wish to be a vegetarian, I do not want to eat meat from animals that have endured a horrible life from start to finish.

Fresh Tomato Juice

SERVES ABOUT 4–6

450g (1lb) very ripe tomatoes, peeled and halved
1 spring onion with a little green leaf or
1 slice onion, 5cm (2in) diameter and
5mm (¼in) thick
3 large basil or 5–6 mint leaves
2 teaspoons white wine vinegar
1 tablespoon olive oil
125ml (4fl oz) water
1 teaspoon salt
1 teaspoon sugar
A few grinds of black pepper

This is only worth making when you have very well-flavoured vine-ripened tomatoes. We make it throughout September when our tomatoes have really developed intense flavour. It is best when freshly made and better not kept for more than 8 hours. It makes a great base for bloody marys or you can sweeten it and freeze it as a granita.

Liquidize the ingredients together, then strain through a nylon sieve. Taste, add more seasoning if necessary. Serve unadorned in tall glasses.

Field Mushroom Soup

SERVES 8–9

115g (4oz) onion
40g (1½oz) butter
450g (1lb) field mushrooms
(*Agaricus campestris*)
Salt and freshly ground black pepper
25g (1oz) flour
600ml (1 pint) Home-made Chicken Stock
(see page 184)
600ml (1 pint) milk
Dash of cream (optional)

Some years pass and not a single mushroom pops up in the fields; in other years they are so abundant that we are frantically making ketchup, sauces, soups and so on to use them up. In fact the base of this recipe is a perfect way to preserve field mushrooms when local children bring us more than we can eat: allow the mixture (without the stock) to cool, then freeze it.

Chop the onion finely. Melt the butter in a saucepan on a gentle heat. Toss the onion in it, cover and sweat until soft and completely cooked. Meanwhile, chop up the mushrooms very finely. (If you can't be bothered to chop the mushrooms finely, just slice and then whizz the soup in a liquidizer for a few seconds after it is cooked.) Add to the saucepan and cook on a high heat for 3–4 minutes. Then stir in the flour and cook on a low heat for 2–3 minutes. Season with salt and pepper, then add the stock and milk gradually, stirring all the time.

Increase the heat and bring to the boil. Taste and add a dash of cream if necessary and serve.

Beetroot Soup with Chive Cream

SERVES 8–10

800g (1³/₄lb) whole beetroot
225g (8oz) onions
25g (1oz) butter
Salt and freshly ground black pepper
About 1.2 litres (2 pints) Home-made
Chicken Stock (see page 184)
Cream

CHIVE CREAM
125ml (4fl oz) softly whipped sour cream
Chives, finely chopped

We love beetroot in all shapes and forms. In the spring we eat them when they are tiny with butter, cream and parsley. We also adore the tiny leaves in salads and use the larger ones as wilted greens with garlic and olive oil. The larger beetroot (Golden Chioggia is an excellent variety) we make into pickles or soups, or simply bake in the oven. One fabulous use for them is to make Crisps (see page 127).

Wash the beetroot carefully under a cold tap. Don't scrub it, simply rub off the soil with your fingers – you don't want to damage the skin or cut off the top or tails because the beetroot will 'bleed' in the cooking. Put the beetroot into boiling water and simmer, covered, for anything from 20 minutes to 2 hours, depending on the size. The beetroot are cooked when the skins will rub off easily.

Meanwhile chop the onions and sweat carefully and gently in the butter until they are cooked. Chop the beetroot and add to the onions. Season with salt and pepper. Put into a liquidizer with the chicken stock. Liquidize until quite smooth. Reheat, add a little cream, taste and adjust the seasoning – it may be necessary to add a little more stock or cream. Serve garnished with swirls of whipped sour cream and a sprinkling of chives.

Pumpkin Soup

SERVES 6–8

900g (2lb) pumpkin flesh
55g (2oz) butter
2 onions, sliced
2 teaspoons marjoram or thyme, freshly
chopped
Salt and freshly ground black pepper
1–1½ tablespoons sugar
600ml (1 pint) milk
About 300ml (½ pint) Home-made Chicken
Stock (see page 184) (optional)

GARNISH

4 streaky bacon rashers
2 tablespoons whipped cream
1 tablespoon chopped parsley

Pumpkins grow so well in our vegetable garden and we harvest them in October and November. We grow several varieties and many kinds of squash, too, so they are used in many more ways than simply becoming lanterns at Hallowe'en.

First prepare the pumpkin. The method you use will depend on how you intend to serve the soup. If you plan to serve it in a tureen or individual soup bowls, simply cut the pumpkin in half or quarters and scoop out the seeds and fibrous matter from the centre. Save the seeds to roast (see below) and nibble as a snack. Peel off the skin with a knife and cut the flesh into cubes.

If, however, you would like to use the pumpkin shell for a more dramatic presentation, then you will need to proceed with care. Slice a 'lid' off the top of the pumpkin and scoop out the seeds and fibrous matter. Then carefully scoop out the pumpkin flesh – a sharp-edged tablespoon is best for this, but be careful not to damage the pumpkin shell. You may need to make double the given quantities of soup to fill the pumpkin tureen.

Next make the soup. Melt the butter in a saucepan; when it foams, add the onions and sweat for a few minutes until soft. Add the chopped pumpkin and coat in the butter. Add the herbs, salt, pepper, sugar and milk, bring to the boil and simmer until the pumpkin is cooked.

Liquidize the mixture, taste and correct the seasoning if necessary. If the soup is a little thick, thin with some boiling chicken stock.

Grill the bacon rashers until they are really crisp, then cut into lardons. Pour the hot soup into a tureen or back into the pumpkin shell and swirl the whipped cream on top. Scatter with crispy bacon and chopped parsley. Serve immediately.

Lydia's Roasted Pumpkin Seeds

Pumpkin seeds
Sea salt

Preheat the oven to 110°C/225°F/gas mark ¼.

Remove all the seeds from the flesh and rinse under cold water. Pat dry on kitchen paper. Lay a single layer on a baking tray and sprinkle generously with sea salt.

Put into the preheated oven for 30–40 minute until the seeds are nice and crunchy. They may be stored, sealed in a tin or a jar.

Fish Mousse with Chanterelles and Chive Butter Sauce

SERVES 16–20

MOUSSE
350g (12oz) very fresh fillets of whiting or pollock, skinned and totally free of bone or membrane
1 teaspoon salt
Pinch of freshly ground white pepper
1 free-range egg
1 free-range egg white
750ml (1¼ pints) cream, chilled

CHIVE BUTTER SAUCE
Beurre Blanc Sauce (recipe x 2) (see page 29)
225–350g (8–12oz) chanterelles
25g (1oz) butter
Salt and freshly ground black pepper
1–2 tablespoons chives, finely chopped

GARNISH
Sprigs of chervil

YOU WILL NEED
16–20 ramekins, 5cm (2in) diameter, 2.5cm (1in) deep, brushed with a little melted butter
Bain-marie

This recipe makes a large number of light fish mousses – it is difficult to reduce the quantities further without upsetting the proportions, so the recipe is perfect for a large dinner party. Even though the mousse is light, it is also very rich, so we cook it in small ramekins. The freshest sweet fish is utterly essential because there is nothing to mask the taint if the fish is even slightly stale. The fish itself does not need to be expensive – we use pollock or whiting. Careful seasoning of the raw mixture is vital. Cooked crab meat, oysters, prawns, shrimps, periwinkles or tiny dice of cucumber could also be added to the Beurre Blanc Sauce.

It is best to have everything well chilled to start with, including the bowl of the food processor. Cut the fish fillets into small dice and purée the pieces in the chilled bowl. Add the salt and pepper, then the egg and egg white; continue to purée until these are well incorporated. Chill in the refrigerator for 30 minutes.

Preheat the oven to 200°C/400°F/gas mark 6.

When the fish has rested for 30 minutes, blend in the cream and whizz again just until it is well incorporated. Check the seasoning. The mousses can be prepared to this point several hours ahead. Cover and refrigerate until needed.

Meanwhile brush the ramekins with melted butter, pop the mousse mixture into the ramekins and put them in a bain-marie. Fill the bain-marie with boiling water – it should come more than halfway up the ramekins. Cover with a pricked sheet of tin foil or greaseproof paper and transfer to the pre-heated oven to bake for about 20 minutes. When cooked the mousses should feel just firm in the centre. They will keep perfectly for 20–30 minutes in a plate-warming oven.

Meanwhile make the Beurre Blanc Sauce in a heatproof bowl. Put the bowl into a saucepan of hot but not simmering water to keep warm.

Wash and slice the chanterelles. Melt the butter over a high heat until it foams. Add the chanterelles and keep the heat turned up until they are cooked through. Season with salt and pepper and add to the Beurre Blanc Sauce with the chives. Taste and correct the seasoning: the sauce should be very thin and light.

To serve: pour a little hot sauce on to each plate, unmould a mousse and place it in the centre. Arrange a few pieces of chanterelle around the wobbly mousse. Spoon a little more sauce over the mousse and serve immediately – they are no longer as delicious if they are allowed to get cold. Garnish with sprigs of chervil.

Oysters Chez Panisse

SERVES 4

A selection of lettuces and salad leaves
16 oysters

LEMON OIL DRESSING
1 large shallot, peeled and finely chopped
1 tablespoon orange juice
1 tablespoon lemon juice
2 tablespoons wine or champagne vinegar
175ml (6fl oz) extra virgin olive oil
Zest of 1/2 lemon
Zest of 1/2 orange
Salt and freshly ground black pepper

Seasoned flour
Beaten egg
White fluffy breadcrumbs
Clarified butter

GARNISH
Snipped flat-leaf parsley

Eddie Walsh, a chef at Ballymaloe House, goes to Chez Panisse in Berkeley, California, every year, to soak up Alice Waters' fresh exciting food philosophy. In the spring he returns to Ireland with his head swirling with ideas; and after one such trip he cooked me these oysters.

Wash and dry the lettuces and salad leaves, then make the dressing. Put the finely chopped shallot into a bowl and add the orange and lemon juice. Season well. Whisk together all the remaining ingredients for the dressing and add to the shallots.

Open the oysters and remove from their shells. Drain in a sieve over a bowl. Just before serving, toss each oyster in seasoned flour, beaten egg and white breadcrumbs. Melt a little clarified butter in a pan and cook the oysters over a moderate heat until crisp and golden on all sides.

Meanwhile toss the salad leaves in just a little dressing. Put a fistful of salad on each plate with four crispy sizzling oysters on top. Sprinkle with snipped flat-leaf parsley and serve immediately.

Mustard Greens

SERVES 6

500g (1lb 2oz) spinach, very finely chopped

500g (1lb 2oz) mustard greens (just leaves with their stems), very finely chopped

5 tablespoons coarsely chopped garlic

4–6 fresh hot green chillies

1¹⁄₂ –2 teaspoons salt

5–6 tablespoons fine cornmeal

3 tablespoons ghee, clarified butter or vegetable oil

1 medium-large onion, about 115g (4oz), finely chopped

5cm (2in) piece of fresh ginger, peeled and cut into thin, long slivers

2 medium-sized, very ripe tomatoes, finely chopped

A generous dollop of unsalted butter

On Madhur Jaffrey's last visit to the school she walked through the vegetable garden with me. She became wildly excited when she spied our exuberant patch of mustard greens cropping so well we could not use them fast enough. Her eyes sparkled as she told me about a wonderful Punjabi recipe she had found for mustard greens – the perfect way to use up some of our abundant crop. It was exquisite – worth growing mustard greens specially. The recipe comes from her book Flavours of India *and I reprint with her kind permission.*

Combine the spinach, mustard greens, garlic, chillies, salt and 800ml (1¹⁄₃ pints) water in a large, heavy pan. Set over high heat and bring to the boil. Cover, turn the heat to low and simmer gently for 1³⁄₄ hours or until even the stems of the mustard green leaves have turned buttery soft. With the heat still on, add 5 tablespoons of the cornmeal, beating constantly with a whisk or a traditional greens masher as you do so. Using the same whisk or masher, mash the greens until they are fairly smooth (a little coarseness is desirable). The greens will thicken with the addition of the cornmeal. If they remain somewhat watery, add another tablespoon or so. Leave on very low heat.

Heat the ghee, clarified butter or oil in a separate pan or wok over medium-high heat. When hot, put in the onion. Stir and fry until it turns golden brown. Add the ginger. Keep stirring and frying until the onion is medium-brown. Put in the tomatoes. Stir and fry until the tomatoes have softened and browned a little. Now pour this mixture over the greens and stir it in. Transfer the greens to a serving dish, top with a dollop of butter and serve.

Right: the potting shed, nestling in the corner here, was derelict when we arrived at Kinoith and had to be reglazed. I have had my eye on the Fernery, next door, as a project ripe for regeneration.

Portobella Mushrooms with Parsley Pesto and Balsamic Vinegar

SERVES 6

6 Portobella mushrooms or large meaty flats

Salt and freshly ground black pepper

2 large cloves crushed garlic

Olive oil

115g (4oz) cooked beetroot

65ml (2¹/₂fl oz) chicken stock or vegetable stock

2 tablespoons cream

65ml (2¹/₂fl oz) balsamic vinegar

Parsley or Basil Pesto (see page 186)

GARNISH

Fresh thyme leaves and edible flowers

If you cannot get Portobellas, use the biggest, fattest meaty mushrooms you can find. As a rule of thumb, mushrooms are often better when they are 4–5 days old, once they have had time to develop their flavour.

Preheat the oven to 250°C/475°F/gas mark 9.

If you are using Portobella mushrooms, split them in half widthways and arrange on a baking tray in a single layer. Flats should be kept whole. Sprinkle with salt, a few grinds of pepper and crushed garlic. Drizzle with olive oil and roast them in the preheated oven for 10–15 minutes or until cooked through.

Purée the beetroot with a little chicken or vegetable stock and cream. Taste and correct the seasoning.

When the mushrooms are almost cooked, reduce the balsamic vinegar in a small saucepan until slightly syrupy. Sandwich the two pieces of each Portobella mushroom together with a dollop of Parsley or Basil Pesto. Arrange each one in the centre of a hot plate. Drizzle balsamic vinegar and beetroot purée around the edge. Garnish with thyme leaves and edible flowers.

111

Spiced Aubergine with Goat's Cheese and Rocket Leaves

SERVES 6

800g (1³/₄lb) aubergines
About 230ml (8fl oz) vegetable oil
(we use arachide)
2.5cm (1in) cube fresh ginger, peeled and
coarsely chopped
6 large garlic cloves, peeled and
coarsely crushed
50ml (1¹/₂fl oz) water
1 teaspoon whole fennel seeds
¹/₂ teaspoon whole cumin seeds
350g (12oz) very ripe tomatoes, peeled
and finely chopped, or 1 x 400g (14oz)
tinned tomatoes plus 1 teaspoon sugar
1 tablespoon coriander seeds, freshly
ground
¹/₄ teaspoon ground turmeric
¹/₃ teaspoon cayenne pepper (more if you
like)
About 1 teaspoon salt

55g (2oz) raisins
85g (3oz) soft goat's cheese (we use
Ardsallagh, or St Tola)
125ml (4fl oz) cream

GARNISH
Rocket leaves

Aubergine plants are quite beautiful and we always grow some in the conservatory. Make sure when you are buying or picking them that the top and the leaves are green and not brown and withered.

It is becoming more and more possible to buy many varieties of aubergine – at the American Farmers' Markets of San Francisco or Berkeley, for instance, you will always find at least three organic varieties for sale. Indian aubergines would be good in this recipe, if you can find them. The spiced aubergine mixture is also good served cold or at room temperature as an accompaniment to cold lamb or pork.

Cut the aubergines into 2cm (³/₄in) thick slices. You will need 12 slices (or 18 if you decide to do triple deckers). Heat 175ml (6fl oz) oil in a deep 25–30cm (10–12in) frying pan. When hot, almost smoking, add a few aubergine slices and cook until golden and tender on both sides. Remove and drain on a wire rack over a baking sheet. Repeat with the remainder of the aubergines, adding more oil if necessary.

Put the ginger, garlic and water into a blender or food processor. Blend until fairly smooth.

Heat the remaining oil in the frying pan. When hot, add the fennel and cumin seeds. (Be careful not to let them burn.) Stir for just a few seconds, then add the chopped tomatoes, the ginger-garlic mixture, coriander, turmeric, cayenne and salt. Simmer, stirring occasionally, until the spice mixture thickens slightly, about 5–6 minutes.

Add the fried aubergine slices and the raisins, and mix gently with the spicy sauce. Cover the pan, reduce the heat to very low and cook for another 5–8 minutes.

Mix the goat's cheese gently with the softly whipped cream. If the goat's cheese is not soft and fresh like the Ardsallagh cheese we buy, it may be necessary to sieve the goat's cheese before gently folding into the cream.

To serve: put one slice of spiced aubergine on to a warm plate and spoon a generous blob of goat's cheese on top. Cover with another slice of aubergine and garnish with a few young rocket leaves and a little cracked pepper. Serve warm.

Crab Cakes with Coriander Cream and Salsa Cruda

SERVES 5–6

425g (15oz) crab meat, brown and white
mixed (2 or 3 crabs should yield this – or
just use white meat if you prefer)
115g (4oz) soft white breadcrumbs
2–3 teaspoons white wine vinegar
2 tablespoons ripe tomato chutney or
Ballymaloe Tomato Relish (which is
now available in many shops)
25g (1oz) softened butter
1 teaspoon dry English mustard powder or
1 rounded teaspoon French mustard
2 tablespoons coriander, freshly chopped
A dash of Tabasco or a good pinch of
cayenne pepper
Salt and freshly ground black pepper
175ml (6fl oz) Béchamel Sauce
(see page 182)
Olive oil

COATING
Seasoned flour
1 free-range egg white, beaten
White breadcrumbs

Salsa Cruda (see page 187)

CORIANDER CREAM
3 tablespoons coriander, freshly chopped
175ml (6fl oz) whipped cream
Salt and freshly ground black pepper
1 teaspoon freshly squeezed lemon juice

GARNISH
Coriander leaves

When I first arrived at Ballymaloe it was a real treat to get crabs. The fishermen would always say that they could not be bothered to bring them in as there was no call for them. We eventually started to say that we would buy the whole catch from them. This was risky because they could bring in three or four or they might bring in thirty to forty, in which case we would set about busily making crab salad, soups and cakes. All around the table the family would be sitting bashing crab claws and salvaging all the beautiful meat. At the last moment my father-in-law, Ivan Allen, would enter the kitchen ceremoniously to dress the crab.

Nowadays crabs are landed regularly and although the prices have rocketed they are still very good value. These crab cakes are based on Ivan Allen's recipe.

Mix all the ingredients for the crab cakes, except the olive oil, in a bowl. Taste carefully and correct the seasoning – it should taste well seasoned and quite perky. Form the mixture into 10–12 cakes. Coat first with seasoned flour, then egg and finally breadcrumbs. Put on to a baking tray lined with silicone paper. Chill until firm.

Meanwhile make the Coriander Cream. Fold the chopped coriander into the whipped cream, add salt, freshly ground pepper and sugar and the lemon juice. Taste and add a little more seasoning if necessary.

To serve: heat good quality oil in a deep-fryer or in a frying pan. Cook the crab cakes until crisp and golden. Drain on kitchen paper and serve immediately on hot plates with a dollop of Coriander Cream and some Salsa Cruda on the side.

Seared Tuna with Piperonata and Tapenade

SERVES 6

6 x 175g (6oz) pieces of tuna
2 tablespoons olive oil
Salt and freshly ground black pepper

Piperonata (see page 128)
Tapenade (see page 187)

GARNISH
6–8 sprigs flat-leaf parsley or basil

Occasionally a tuna is caught off Ballycotton – great excitement! The secret of cooking tuna is to underdo it, like a rare steak, so that it is moist and juicy; well cooked it can become dry and dull. The sweetness of Piperonata and the gutsy taste of Tapenade are great with it.

First make the Piperonata and the Tapenade.

Preheat the grill pan. Brush the tuna with oil and season well with salt and pepper. Sear the tuna on the hot grill pan, turning it first in one direction and then the other, so that it develops a grid pattern from the ridges of the pan. Cook on both sides for 2–3 minutes. The centre should still be 'pink'.

Meanwhile reheat the Piperonata if necessary. Put a few tablespoons on each plate and place a piece of sizzling tuna on top. Put a little Tapenade on top or dot irregularly around the edge of the Piperonata. Add a few sprigs of flat-leaf parsley or basil and serve immediately.

Poached Grey Sea Mullet with Hollandaise and Pea and Parsley Champ

SERVES 4

1 grey sea mullet
Water
Salt (see method)

Hollandaise Sauce (see page 182)

Pea and Parsley Champ (see page 126)

GARNISH
Segments of lemon
Fresh herbs, such as chervil, fennel or flat-leaf parsley

Some people may feel, wrongly, that Hollandaise Sauce is old hat but our version, made without being reduced, with fine Irish butter, is completely exquisite. We serve it with poached fresh bass, salmon, or, in this case, grey sea mullet. The sauce turns this underrated fish into an absolute feast. It is particularly delicious with soft and melting Pea and Parsley Champ.

Gut, scale and clean the grey sea mullet, removing the head if you prefer – a slightly gory business which you might want to ask your fishmonger to do if you are squeamish.

Choose a saucepan that just fits the fish or better still use a small fish kettle. Measure the water carefully and add 1 rounded tablespoon of salt to every 1.2 litres (2 pints) water. Cover the saucepan or kettle and bring the water to the boil. Put in the fish, which should be just covered with water. Replace the lid on the saucepan, bring back to the boil and simmer for 10 minutes only.

Meanwhile make the Hollandaise Sauce.

Test the fish – it is cooked if the flesh comes away from the backbone close to the head when you lift it with the tip of a knife; if there is still resistance, replace the lid and leave the fish sitting in the water for a few more minutes.

To serve: put the fish on a hot serving dish and garnish with segments of lemon and fresh herbs. At the table lift off the skin and put a portion of fish on to each plate, coat with the Hollandaise sauce and eat immediately with Pea and Parsley Champ. This fish is also lovely with Beurre Blanc (see page 29).

Warm Poached Mackerel with Bretonne Sauce

SERVES 4

4 very fresh mackerel
1.2 litres (2 pints) water
1 teaspoon salt

BRETONNE SAUCE
55g (2oz) butter, melted
2 egg yolks, preferably free-range
1 teaspoon Dijon mustard (we use Maille Verte aux Herbes)
¹/₂ teaspoon white wine vinegar
1 tablespoon chopped parsley or a mixture of chopped chervil, chives, tarragon and fennel

'The sun should never set on a mackerel', Tommy Sliney, the much-loved Ballycotton fish trader once told me, because within 5 hours the oil in the fish turns bitter. Really fresh mackerel, gently poached and served warm with this simple sauce, is an absolute feast and without question one of my favourite foods. Anyone who wonders why I get so excited about mackerel has not tasted it this way!

Cut the heads off the mackerel. Gut and clean them but keep whole. Bring the water to the boil and add the salt and the mackerel. Cover, bring back to boiling point, then remove from the heat. After about 5–8 minutes, check to see whether the fish are cooked. The flesh should lift off the bone. It will be tender and melting.

Meanwhile make the sauce. Melt the butter and allow to boil. Put the egg yolks into a heat-proof bowl. Add the mustard, wine vinegar and herbs and mix well. Whisk the hot melted butter into the egg yolk mixture little by little so that the sauce emulsifies. Keep warm, by placing the heatproof bowl in a saucepan of hot but not boiling water.

When the mackerel is cool enough to handle, remove to a plate. Skin, lift the flesh carefully from the bones and arrange on a serving dish. Coat with the sauce and serve while still warm with a good green salad and new potatoes.

Roast Guinea-fowl with Parsnip Crisps and Redcurrant Sauce

SERVES 4

1 guinea-fowl
A little softened or melted butter

STUFFING
40g (1¹/₂oz) butter
85g (3oz) chopped onions
65g (2¹/₂oz) breadcrumbs
1 tablespoon freshly chopped herbs, such as parsley, thyme, chives and marjoram
Salt and freshly ground black pepper

Parsnip Crisps (see page 127)
Redcurrant Sauce (see page 187)

Game or Home-made Chicken Stock (see page 184)

GARNISH
Sprigs of watercress

James Veale rears plump guinea-fowl for us which have a superb flavour. We used to keep guinea-fowls ourselves, but the 'gebak, gebak, gebak' noise which they make frightened my chickens and Frank complained that they had been put off laying. One night the guinea-fowl all disappeared – I didn't ask what happened to them...

Preheat the oven to 190°C/375°F/gas mark 5.

Gut the guinea-fowl if necessary and remove the 'crop' which is at the neck end; wash and dry well.

To make the stuffing, melt the butter and sweat the onions until soft but not coloured, then remove from the heat. Stir in the soft white breadcrumbs and freshly chopped herbs, season with salt and pepper and taste. Unless you are going to cook the bird right away, let the stuffing become quite cold before putting it into the bird.

Season the cavity with salt and pepper and stuff the guinea-fowl loosely. Smear the breast and legs with softened or melted butter. Roast in the pre-heated oven for about 1¹/₄ hours. Test by pricking the leg at the thickest point: the juices should just run clear.

Meanwhile make the Redcurrant Sauce and the Parsnip Crisps.

Spoon off any surplus fat from the roasting pan (keep it for roasting or sautéing potatoes).

Deglaze the pan with game or chicken stock. Bring it to the boil and use a whisk to dislodge the crusty caramelized juices so they can dissolve into the gravy. Season with salt and pepper, taste and boil until you are happy with the flavour. Pour into a hot sauce-boat.

Carve the guinea-fowl into four portions, giving each person some brown and some white meat. Spoon a little gravy over the meat. Pile some Parsnip Crisps over the top. Garnish with large sprigs of watercress and serve with Redcurrant Sauce.

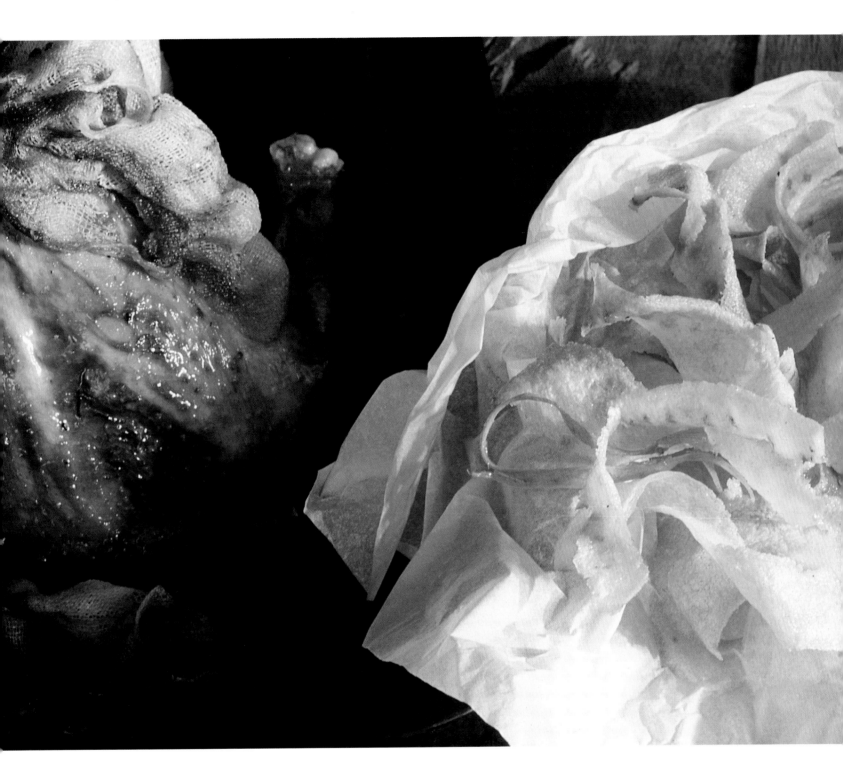

Char-grilled Sirloin Steak with Salsa Verde and Rustic Roast Potatoes

SERVES 2

2 x 175g (6oz) sirloin or 1 x 5cm (2in) thick rib steak

Salsa Verde (see page 187)

RUSTIC ROAST POTATOES
900g (2lb) small new potatoes
1 clove of garlic
Extra virgin olive oil
Freshly ground black pepper

SALAD AND DRESSING
2 bunches rocket, watercress or mixed lettuces
1 tablespoon red wine vinegar
3 tablespoons extra virgin olive oil
Sea salt and freshly ground black pepper

This was cooked for me by my great friend Mary Risley, who owns the highly acclaimed Tante Marie Cooking School in San Francisco. Char-grilled steak has a wonderful flavour, but an iron grill pan also gives a delicious result.

Preheat the oven to 220°C/435°F/gas mark 7.

Wash the potatoes and rub with olive oil. Sprinkle with salt and freshly ground pepper. Put the potatoes on a baking sheet and roast in the pre-heated oven until crispy and tender – about 35 minutes.

To prepare the steak, rub both sides with a cut clove of garlic, drizzle with extra virgin olive oil and sprinkle with pepper. Leave at room temperature for at least 30 minutes.

Meanwhile make the Salsa Verde.

At the last minute, salt the steak on both sides, grill over a charcoal fire or on a grill pan, then leave to relax for 5 minutes on a wooden board.

Put the rocket leaves, watercress sprigs or salad leaves into a bowl. Mix the red wine vinegar with the extra virgin olive oil. Season well with salt and pepper. Toss the salad in a little dressing, just enough to make the leaves glisten. Arrange on a serving plate. Pop the roast potatoes around the sides. Slice the steak thickly at an angle. Arrange the slices of steak over the salad and drizzle the Salsa Verde over the meat.

Roast Pork with Crackling and Spiced Aubergines

I dispair of the flavour of intensively reared animals, quite apart from my unease over their welfare. We rear our own or get our meat from Seamus Hogan, a poet and farmer from Kanturk, County Cork, or our neighbour Patty Walsh. Their pork is so juicy it has you licking your fingers. You will most certainly need to order your joint in advance to ensure that the rind is still on – no rind, no crackling!

SERVES 10–12

1 x 2.25kg (5lb) loin of pork with the rind intact

Salt and freshly ground black pepper

2 tablespoons mixed fresh herbs (such as parsley, thyme, chives, marjoram, savory, perhaps a little sage or rosemary)

Spiced Aubergine mixture (see page 112) (use up to twice the amount in the recipe, depending on your appetite)

Lentilles du Puy (see page 131)

Preheat the oven to 190°C/375°F/gas mark 5.

Score the skin at 5mm (¹/₄in) intervals running with the grain – ask your butcher to do this if possible because the rind, particularly of free-range pork, can be quite tough. This is to give you really good crackling and make it easier to carve later.

Put the pork, skin-side down, on a chopping board, season with salt and pepper and sprinkle with freshly chopped herbs. Roll up tightly and tie with cotton string. Sprinkle some salt over the rind, roast the joint on a wire rack in a roasting tin in the preheated oven. Allow 25–28 minutes for each 450g (1lb). Baste with the rendered pork fat every now and then.

Meanwhile cook the Spiced Aubergines and Lentilles du Puy.

Just before the end of the cooking time, transfer the pork to another roasting tin. Return the meat to the oven and increase the temperature to 230°C/450°F/gas mark 8 to crisp the crackling further.

When the joint is cooked, the juices should run clear, Put the pork on to a hot carving dish and leave to rest for 10–15 minutes in a low oven before carving. Serve with the Spiced Aubergine and the Lentilles du Puy. Roast potatoes and a green salad would also make a good accompaniment.

Glazed Loin of Bacon with Tomato Fondue and Scallion Champ

SERVES 12–15

1.8–2.25kg (4–5lb) loin of bacon, smoked or unsmoked complete with rind and a nice layer of fat
About 20–30 whole cloves
350g (12oz) brown demerara sugar
3–4 tablespoons pineapple juice from a small tin

Tomato Fondue (see page 182)

Scallion Champ (see page 40)

Irish bacon has quite a different flavour from that of other countries. When you can buy it with a nice layer of fat it has a sweet, juicy flavour. Yet so strong is the predominant dietary fear that most consumers ask for meat with no fat at all! This makes no sense, either from the culinary or the health angle, and I lose sleep trying to work out how to get this simple message across, now that people have been led to believe that fat is public enemy number one!

The bacon should be cooked with the rind on to keep in the flavour and give a good surface to glaze. Bacon is one of the traditional flavours of Ireland that we serve with pride to our guests.

Cover the bacon in cold water and bring slowly to the boil. If the bacon is very salty, a white froth forms on top of the water, in which case it is best to discard the water. It may be necessary to change the water several times depending on how salty the bacon is. Finally, cover it with hot water and simmer until almost cooked, allowing about 20 minutes to each 450g (1lb).

Preheat the oven to 250°C/475°F/gas mark 9.

Remove the rind carefully – it will peel off in a sheet. Score the fat into a diamond pattern and stud with cloves. Mix the brown sugar to a thick paste with a little pineapple juice – be careful not to make it too liquid. Spread this paste over the bacon fat. Put into a low-sided ovenproof dish just large enough to fit the joint.

Bake in the preheated oven for about 20–30 minutes or until the top has caramelized. Spoon the glaze up over the bacon several times during this period and keep an eye on it. At first nothing much happens, but once the glaze heats up it can caramelize very quickly and within minutes turn black and acrid – believe me, I know from experience!

Serve with Tomato Fondue and Scallion Champ.

Tarragon Chicken with Chilli and Tomato Fondue

SERVES 4–6

1 x 1.25kg (3¼lb) chicken (free-range if possible)
Salt and freshly ground black pepper
1 tablespoon freshly chopped French tarragon, and sprig of tarragon
20g (¾oz) butter
150ml (¼ pint) Home-made Chicken Stock, optional (see page 184)
150ml (¼ pint) cream
½–1 tablespoon freshly chopped French tarragon (for the sauce)
Roux (optional) (see page 182)

Chilli and Tomato Fondue (see page 130)

GARNISH
Sprigs of tarragon

YOU WILL NEED
1 x 2.4 litre (4 pint) ovenproof casserole

Tarragon Chicken is a great classic and this method of cooking chicken inside a casserole preserves the juices. It is also a splendid way to cook pheasant, turkey and guinea-fowl. Vary the herbs: marjoram is good too.

Preheat the oven to 180°C/350°F/gas mark 4.

Remove the wing tips and wishbone from the chicken and keep for making stock. Season the cavity of the chicken with salt and pepper. Stuff a sprig of tarragon inside – this will perfume the chicken flesh as it cooks. Chop the remaining tarragon and mix with two-thirds of the butter. Smear the remaining butter over the breast of the chicken. A 2.2-litre (4-pint) oval casserole is the perfect size for the recipe.

Place the chicken breast-side down in the casserole and let it brown over a gentle heat. This may take up to 6–7 minutes – don't hurry it or you may burn the bottom of the casserole and spoil the flavour of the sauce later. Turn the chicken breast-side up and smear the tarragon butter over the breast and legs. Season with salt and pepper. Cover the casserole and put into the preheated oven for 1¼ –1½ hours. To test if the chicken is cooked, pierce the flesh between the breast and thigh. This is the last place to cook, so if there is no trace of pink here and if the juices are clear, the chicken is certainly cooked.

Meanwhile make the Chilli and Tomato Fondue.

Remove the chicken to a carving dish, keep warm and let it rest while you make the sauce. Spoon every scrap of fat from the juices and add the stock, cream and a little freshly chopped tarragon. Boil until the sauce thickens slightly.

Alternatively, bring the liquid to the boil, and whisk in just enough Roux to thicken the sauce to a light coating consistency. Taste and add a little more seasoning and chopped tarragon if necessary. If the sauce is thickened with Roux, this dish may be reheated.

Carve the chicken into 4–6 portions; each person should have some white and some brown meat. Arrange on a serving dish, coat with the sauce and serve immediately with the Chilli and Tomato Fondue.

Hamburgers with Ginger Mushrooms and Buffalo Chips

SERVES 4–6

15g (¹/₂oz) butter
85g (3oz) onion, finely chopped
450g (1lb) freshly minced beef – flank, chump or shin would be perfect
¹/₂ teaspoon fresh thyme leaves
¹/₂ teaspoon fresh parsley, finely chopped
1 egg, preferably free-range, beaten
Salt and freshly ground black pepper
Pork caul fat (optional)

Ginger Mushrooms (see page 130)

BUFFALO CHIPS
6 large potatoes, unpeeled
Salt
Oil for deep-frying – olive or a mixture of olive and sunflower

Oil for frying

Dressed green salad, 1–2 cherry tomatoes and 1 spring onion (optional) per person

This scrummy combination is one of Timmy's specialities, adored and much requested by the children, their friends, and me too!.

First make the hamburgers. Melt the butter in a saucepan, toss in the chopped onion and sweat until soft but not coloured; then leave to get cold. Mix the minced beef with the herbs and beaten egg, season with salt and pepper, add the onion and mix well. Fry a tiny bit in the pan, taste to check the seasoning and adjust if necessary. Then shape into hamburgers, 4–6 depending on the size you require. Wrap each one loosely in caul fat if using. Keep refrigerated.

Next make the Ginger Mushrooms and keep aside.

Scrub the potatoes and cut into wedges from top to bottom – they should be about 2cm (³/₄in) thick and at least 6.5cm (2¹/₂in) long. If you like, rinse the chips quickly in cold water but do not soak; dry them meticulously with a tea towel or kitchen paper before cooking. Heat the oil in the deep-fryer to 180°C/350°F. You need to fry the chips twice, first at this temperature for 5–8 minutes depending on size, then drain.

Next fry the hamburgers and reheat the Ginger Mushrooms. Increase the heat in the deep-fryer to 220°C/425°F and cook the Buffalo Chips again, for 1–2 minutes, until crisp and golden. Shake the basket and drain the chips well. Toss on to kitchen paper and sprinkle with salt.

Put the hamburgers on to hot plates, spoon some Ginger Mushrooms over the side of the hamburgers and pile on the crispy Buffalo Chips. Put a little green salad dressed in a well flavoured dressing on the side with one or two cherry tomatoes and a perky spring onion.

Aileen's Papardelle with Roast Pumpkin, Pine Kernels and Rocket Leaves

A gorgeous autumn pasta dish conjured up by Aileen Murphy, one of the bright young chefs in the Ballymaloe kitchen. We use the basic idea of the recipe in many ways during the rest of the year adding eveything from fresh asparagus, roast yellow peppers and pine kernels to rocket and broad beans and a sprinkling of Parmesan.

SERVES 4

225g (8oz) wedge of pumpkin
Salt and freshly ground black pepper
Melted butter
2 tablespoons pine kernels
230ml (8fl oz) cream
40g (1¹/₂oz) butter
75g (2¹/₂oz) Parmesan cheese,
freshly grated (Parmigiano Reggiano is
best)
Grating of nutmeg
4.5 litres (8 pints) water
450g (1lb) fresh papardelle
16–24 rocket leaves, depending on size –
ours are often quite big – reserving a
few as a garnish
Extra freshly grated Parmesan

Preheat the oven to 180°C/350°F/gas mark 4.

Season the pumpkin with salt and pepper. Drizzle with melted butter, cover loosely with tin foil and roast in the preheated oven for 25 minutes, or until the pumpkin is tender. Cut into 2.5cm (1in) cubes and keep warm. Toast the pine kernels until golden, either in the oven or under a grill.

Put the cream and butter in a saucepan and simmer over medium heat for less than a minute, by which time the butter and cream will have slightly thickened. Add the Parmesan, salt, pepper and a grating of nutmeg. Remove from the heat and set aside for a few minutes until required.

Bring a large saucepan of water to the boil, add 2 tablespoons salt and cook the pasta for 2–3 minutes. Drain.

While the pasta is cooking, reheat the sauce gently and add the cubed pumpkin and the toasted pine kernels.

Drain the pasta and toss carefully in the sauce. Taste and correct the seasoning. Finally, add most of the rocket leaves and allow to wilt slightly. Serve immediately in preheated pasta dishes. Sprinkle with the extra Parmesan cheese and the rest of the fresh rocket leaves as a garnish.

Leek Champ

SERVES 4-6

6–8 unpeeled 'old' potatoes, such as
Golden Wonder or Kerr's Pink
4 medium-sized leeks
40g (1½oz) butter
Salt and freshly ground black pepper
1 tablespoon water, if necessary
300–350ml (10–12fl oz) milk
1 tablespoon chopped chives
About 55g (2oz) butter

I have converted many people who cannot bear boiled leeks with this delicious dish. I found this recipe when I was researching my Irish Traditional Food *book. It is one of many versions of champ and comes from Ulster.*

Scrub the potatoes, cover with cold water and boil them in their skins. Halfway through cooking, pour off half the water, cover the pan and steam until fully cooked.

Cut off the dark green leaves from the top of the leeks (wash and add to the stock-pot or use for making green leek soup). Slit the leeks about halfway down the centre and wash well under cold running water. Slice into 5mm (¼in) rounds. Melt the butter in a heavy saucepan; when it foams, add the sliced leeks and toss gently to coat with butter. Season with salt and pepper and add the water if necessary. Cover with a circle of greaseproof paper and a close-fitting saucepan lid. Reduce the heat and cook very gently for 10–15 minutes, or until soft, tender and juicy. Check and stir every now and then during cooking.

Bring the milk to the boil with the chives and simmer for 3–4 minutes; then turn off the heat and leave to infuse. Peel and mash the freshly boiled potatoes and while hot, mix with the boiling milk and chives, add the drained leeks and beat in the butter. Season to taste with salt and pepper. It should be soft and melting.

Leek Champ may be put aside and reheated later in a preheated oven at 180°C/350°F/gas mark 4. Cover with tin foil while it reheats so that it does not get a skin over the top.

Pea and Parsley Champ

SERVES 4

900g (2lb) 'old' potatoes, such as Golden
Wonder or Kerr's Pink
Salt and freshly ground black pepper
300ml (½ pint) milk
225g (8oz) young peas (shelled weight)
8 tablespoons chopped parsley
25–55g (1–2oz) butter
(traditionally, strong country butter
would have been used)

Another version of the traditional Irish champ – again from Ulster.

Scrub the potatoes, put into a saucepan and cook in their skins in boiling salted water until tender. Drain thoroughly and dry over the heat in the saucepan for a few minutes. Mash the potatoes while hot.

Meanwhile bring the milk to the boil and add the peas. Simmer until the peas are just cooked – allow about 8–10 minutes. Drop in the chopped parsley for the final 2 minutes of cooking. Add the hot milk mixture to the potatoes. Season well, add butter to taste and beat until light and fluffy. The texture should be soft and moist. Serve hot.

Parsnip Crisps

SERVES 6–8

1 large parsnip, sliced or peeled in long slivers, and left to dry for an hour (other root vegetables can also be used)
Sunflower or groundnut oil
Salt

We serve these delicious crisps on warm salads, as a garnish for roast pheasant or guinea-fowl and as a topping for parsnip or other root vegetable soup. Delicious crisps may be made from other vegetables apart from the much-loved potato; celeriac, beetroot, leek and even carrots are also good. The drier the slices the better.

Heat good-quality oil in a deep-fryer to 200°C/400°F. Scrub and peel the parsnips. Either slice into wafer-thin rounds or peel off long slivers length-ways with a swivel-top peeler. Drop a few at a time into the hot oil; they colour and crisp up very quickly. Drain on kitchen paper and sprinkle lightly with salt.

Patty Pan Squash with Basil or Marjoram

SERVES 6

12–18 little patty pan squash or a mixture of patty pan squash and small green zucchini
Olive oil
Salt and freshly ground black pepper
2 tablespoons torn basil leaves or freshly chopped marjoram
A few drops of lemon juice (optional)

When I first grew patty pan squash in the vegetable garden, I waited eagerly for them to crop. I tasted, full of anticipation but, sadly, they are disappointing from the flavour angle. Nonetheless, they look adorable, have beautiful blossoms, and take on other flavours readily. Also, the more you pick, the more they come! They are great with Chilli and Tomato Fondue (see page 130).

Trim the patty pan squash and cut each one into six or eight pie-shaped pieces depending on size. Cut the zucchini if using, on the diagonal into 7mm (1/3in) slices.

Heat a few tablespoons of olive oil in an iron pan or wok and add the patty pan squash and sliced courgettes, if using. Season with salt and pepper and toss rapidly over the heat. Add the torn or chopped herbs and toss for another minute or so. Taste and correct the seasoning – maybe a few drops of lemon juice might be good. Serve immediately.

Fresh Sweetcorn with Marjoram

SERVES 6

6 cobs of corn, preferably freshly picked
Salt and freshly ground black pepper
25–55g (1–2oz) butter
1–2 tablespoons freshly chopped
annual marjoram

This is Timmy's combination, and the freshest sweetcorn is essential. We are lucky because we can pick ours in the garden and rush it to the table.

Bring a large saucepan of water to the boil. Meanwhile, peel the cobs and trim both ends. When the water is boiling, add some salt and the cobs. Cover the saucepan and bring back to the boil; cook for just 3 minutes.

Drain the cobs and leave to cool, then slice the kernels off each cob. Melt a little butter in a saucepan. Add the corn and season with salt and pepper. Add the marjoram and stir once or twice. Taste and correct the seasoning. Serve immediately.

Piperonata

SERVES 8–10

1 onion, sliced
1 clove garlic, crushed
2 red peppers
2 green peppers
6 large, very ripe tomatoes
2 tablespoons extra virgin olive oil
Salt and freshly ground black pepper
Sugar
A few leaves of fresh basil

This is one of the indispensable trio of vegetable stews that we always reckon to have to hand. We use it not only as a vegetable but also as a topping for pizzas, as a sauce for pasta, grilled fish or meat and as a filling for omelettes and pancakes. you can vary the herbs or add some chilli or use all red peppers.

Heat the olive oil in a flameproof casserole. Add the sliced onion, stir and cook for a few seconds; then add the crushed garlic, toss well and allow to soften over a gentle heat in the covered casserole while the peppers are being prepared.

Halve the peppers, remove the seeds carefully, cut into quarters and then into strips across rather than lengthways. The onion should be soft and tender by now so add the peppers and toss well; replace the lid and continue to cook.

Meanwhile peel the tomatoes (scald in boiling water for 10 seconds, pour off the water and peel immediately). Slice the tomatoes and add to the casserole, season with salt, pepper, sugar and a few leaves of fresh basil. Cook gently until the vegetables are just soft – about 30 minutes.

Stir-fried Zucchini with Garlic and Ginger

We grow lots and lots of zucchini and we need endless recipes to use them up. We often toss zucchini prepared like this into pasta and tear in some blossom at the last minute.

SERVES 6

675g (1¹/₂lb) small zucchini, each about 15cm (6in) long
Salt
3 tablespoons olive oil
2 cloves garlic, peeled and mashed
1 tablespoon peeled and grated fresh ginger root
Lots of freshly ground black pepper

Top and tail the zucchini. Cut crosswise into 5mm (¹/₄in) slices. If the zucchini are large, cut each in half lengthways. Using a teaspoon or small melon baller, scrape away all the seeds. Then cut the zucchini crossways into 5mm (¹/₄in) slices. Put in a bowl or colander, sprinkle lightly with salt and mix well. Set aside for 20 minutes. Drain and pat dry.

Heat a wok or cast-iron frying pan over high heat. When it is hot, pour in the oil. Add the garlic and ginger. Stir once or twice and put in the zucchini immediately. Continue to toss over the heat for about 3–4 minutes. The zucchini should not be allowed to get limp. Add freshly ground black pepper, taste and serve immediately.

Ginger Mushrooms

SERVES 6

15–25g (¹/₂–1oz) butter
85g (3oz) onion, finely chopped
225g (8oz) mushrooms
Salt and freshly ground black pepper
A squeeze of lemon juice
125ml (4fl oz) cream
1 teaspoon freshly grated ginger
20g (³/₄oz) nibbed almonds, lightly toasted
¹/₂ tablespoon freshly chopped parsley
¹/₂ tablespoon freshly chopped chives

Melt the butter in a heavy-bottomed saucepan until it foams. Add the chopped onions, cover and sweat on a gentle heat for 5–6 minutes or until quite soft but not coloured. Meanwhile, slice and cook the mushrooms in a hot frying pan in batches if necessary. Season each batch with salt, pepper and a tiny squeeze of lemon juice. Add the mushrooms to the onions in the saucepan, then add the cream, ginger and almonds and allow to bubble for a few minutes. Taste and correct the seasoning; add parsley and chives if used.

Timmy's Chilli and Tomato Fondue

SERVES 4–6

115g (4oz) onions, sliced
1 clove garlic, crushed
1 dessertspoon olive oil
4 large Hungarian Wax chillies
450g (1lb) very ripe tomatoes (or in winter use canned)
Salt, freshly ground pepper and sugar
1 tablespoon chopped herbs such as thyme, parsley, annual marjoram

Lots of chopped fresh coriander

Hungarian Wax, the variety of chilli Timmy uses for his Fondue, is about 18cm (5in) long – sweet and not too hot. Leave the seeds in for extra kick.

Sweat the sliced onions and the garlic in oil over a gentle heat for abut 10 minutes, then add the sliced chillies and continue to sweat until soft. It is vital for the success of this dish that the onions are completely soft before the tomatoes are added. If you are using fresh tomatoes, remove the hard core from the tomatoes. Put them into a deep bowl and cover them with boiling water. Count to 10 and then pour off the water immediately. Peel off the skins, slice and add to the onions and chillies. Season with salt, pepper and sugar and add a generous sprinkling of chopped herbs. Cook for 10–20 minutes more, or until the tomato softens. Add lots of chopped coriander just before serving.

Pink Fir Apple Potatoes

SERVES 2–4

450g (1lb) Pink Fir Apple potatoes
Maldon sea salt
Butter

These are one of many old varieties that we grow every year in the garden. Pink Fir Apple potatoes are waxy in texture, so are good for potato salad.

Scrub the potatoes thoroughly. Boil in well-salted water until cooked through – about 15–20 minutes. Serve immediately with sea salt and lots of butter. We sometimes cut them lengthways and toss them in butter or extra virgin olive oil and sea salt before serving.

Lentilles du Puy

SERVES 4–6

225g (8oz) lentilles du Puy
1 carrot
1 onion, stuck with 2 cloves
Bouquet herbs
Butter or extra virgin olive oil
Lots of freshly squeezed lemon juice
About 2 tablespoons of chopped
fresh herbs (such as oregano,
annual marjoram or parsley)
Sea salt and freshly ground black pepper

Green speckled lentilles du Puy are the aristocrats of the lentil family. They cook in minutes and can play a starring or supporting role in many meals.

Wash the lentils and put into a large saucepan. Fill with cold water, add the carrot, onion and bouquet garni. Bring slowly to the boil, reduce the heat and simmer very gently for 10–15 minutes, testing regularly. The lentils should be *al dente* but not hard. Drain, remove and discard the carrot, onion and bouquet herbs. Season the lentils while warm with a good knob of butter or some extra virgin olive oil, then add lots of freshly squeezed lemon juice and some finely chopped herbs. Season with sea salt and freshly ground black pepper. Serve immediately.

Note: lentils are also good with a little finely chopped chilli added. Add the quantity you like – say half a small chilli with the seeds removed.

Autumn Leaves with Chocolate Mousse

SERVES 8–10

CHOCOLATE MOUSSE
85g (3oz) best quality plain chocolate
25g (1oz) unsweetened chocolate
3 tablespoons dark rum
1 tablespoon cold water
8g ($^{1}/_{4}$oz) powdered gelatine
2 tablespoons water
5 eggs, preferably free-range
75g (2$^{1}/_{2}$oz) caster sugar
350ml (12fl oz) softly whipped cream

CHOCOLATE LEAVES
White chocolate
Plain chocolate
Milk chocolate
Interestingly shaped leaves, such as
maple, Spanish chestnut and rose
Softly whipped cream

DECORATION
Icing sugar
Unsweetened cocoa powder

I first ate something like this at the Clarence Hotel in Dublin in the 'tea-rooms'. I thought that it was such a fun idea that I re-created it later at home. Choose large, well-veined leaves and always use a good chocolate which has a high percentage of cocoa solids (avoid chocolate made with vegetable fat as it tastes inferior). We use the Lesmé, Callebaut and Valrhona brands.

First make the chocolate mousse. Put the plain and unsweetened chocolate, rum and 1 tablespoon water in a saucepan and melt over a low heat. Put the gelatine in a small heatproof bowl and sponge with 2 tablespoons water, then dissolve over a saucepan of boiling water. Beat three eggs and two yolks with the sugar to a stiff mousse. Add a few tablespoons of this mixture to the gelatine, stir well and then mix with the rest.

Whip the two remaining egg whites stiffly. Fold the chocolate into the mousse, followed quickly by the softly whipped cream and stiffly beaten egg white. The mousse sets very quickly once the chocolate is mixed with the gelatine, so speed is of the essence. Put into individual moulds to set or pour into a shallow dish so it can be scooped out later. Chill the mousse for several hours.

To make the leaves, melt the white, plain and milk chocolates gently in separate heatproof bowls in a very low oven or over simmering water. Paint the chocolate over the undersides of the leaves using the back of a teaspoon or a flat pastry brush. Be careful not to let the chocolate dribble over the edges, otherwise the leaves will be difficult to peel later. Leave to set on silicone paper in a cool place. Make a mixture of colours, shapes and sizes. When the chocolate is set and firm, peel the leaves off carefully. If you are in a hurry, you can speed up the setting process by putting the leaves into the refrigerator, but this does dull the chocolate somewhat.

To assemble: put one unmoulded chocolate mousse or a scoop of the mixture on to a chilled white plate. Decorate with overlapping chocolate leaves, sprinkle with a little icing sugar and unsweetened cocoa powder. Serve immediately.

Yoghurt with Apple Blossom Honey and Toasted Hazelnuts

About 1 tablespoon sweet-tasting hazelnuts
Best quality natural yoghurt, or a goat's milk yoghurt
About 2 tablespoons apple blossom honey or strongly flavoured local honey

We have just two beehives down at the end of the orchard. Some years, if the weather is inclement, we get very few sections but in 1996 my bees produced 'twice the national average', I was pleased as Punch. Although the orchard is five acres of mixed Worcester Pearmain, Bramley Seedling and Grenadier, I don't suppose the honey is totally from the apple blossom but it must be predominantly so – in any case, it tastes wonderful. In autumn we are fortunate to be able to gather our own hazelnuts from the nut walk planted by Lydia Strangman at the beginning of the twentieth century.

We use a superb sheep's milk yoghurt made by Oliver Jungwirth on Manch Farm in West Cork, from the milk of their organically reared Friesland sheep. It comes in dark glass jars to preserve the vitamins and minerals – more expensive than other yoghurt but worth every penny.

Preheat the oven to 200°C/400°F/gas mark 6.

Put the hazelnuts on a baking tray and pop into the preheated oven for 8–10 minutes until the skins loosen. Remove from the oven and as soon as they are cool enough to handle and rub off the thin papery skins. (I usually put them into a tea towel, gather up the edges like a pouch, rub the towel against the nuts for a minute or so and, hey presto, virtually all the skins come off in one go.) If the nuts are still very pale, put them back into the oven for a few more minutes until pale golden and crisp. Chop coarsely.

Just before serving, spoon a generous portion of chilled natural yoghurt on a cold plate, drizzle generously with really good honey and sprinkle with the toasted hazelnuts. Eat immediately.

Roast Crimson Bramleys with Soft Brown Sugar and Cream

SERVES 6

6 Crimson Bramley apples
About 6 tablespoons granulated sugar
6 tablespoons butter
Softly whipped cream
Soft brown (Barbados) sugar

Granpoppy, my maternal grandfather, loved his food. He kept ducks, geese and chickens for the table. The orchard contained many old varieties of apple, and one I particularly remember was a Crimson Bramley, sometimes made into tarts by my grandmother or served as a fluffy apple sauce with roast duck or goose. Granpoppy's favourite, though, was roast apples, which he ate almost every evening throughout the autumn. We have just one tree of Crimson Bramleys; some seasons the apples colour to a rich crimson and other years they are paler. I have never quite discovered why.

Preheat the oven to 200°C/400°F/gas mark 6.

Core the apples cleanly and score the skin around the 'equator'. Put the apples side by side in an ovenproof dish. Fill the centres with a generous tablespoon of sugar and put a generous dab of butter on top. Pour a little water into the base of the dish – about 5mm (1/4in) will be enough. Cover with a sheet of greaseproof paper.

Roast in the preheated oven for about 45 minutes. The cooking time will depend on the size of the apples. They are ready to eat when they are soft, fluffy and bursting out of their jackets.

Genteel people sometimes feel they ought not to allow the apples to burst, but they are immeasurably better when they do. Serve immediately, as they soon collapse and look sad and wizened.Softly whipped cream and a generous sprinkling of soft brown sugar completes the feast.

MAKES 9–10

SYRUP
225g (8oz) sugar
225ml (8fl oz) water
4 sprigs fresh mint
2 teaspoons Liqueur de Framboises
1 tablespoon freshly squeezed lemon juice
3 rounded teaspoons powdered gelatine
3 tablespoons water
450g (1lb) fresh autumn raspberries

MINT CREAM
About 15 mint leaves
1 tablespoon lemon juice
150ml (¼ pint) cream

DECORATION
Mint leaves
Rapberries

YOU WILL NEED
9–10 round moulds – 90ml (3fl oz)
capacity, 6.5cm (2½in) inside diameter,
3cm (1¼in) deep

Autumn Raspberry Jellies with Fresh Mint Cream

We use our Heritage variety of autumn raspberry which bears fruit until December. They are slow to ripen but this means their flavour is more intense, and we really value their long season. These fresh-tasting jellies are the perfect finale to a rich meal.

Prepare the syrup by bringing the sugar, water and mint leaves to the boil slowly. Simmer for a few minutes. Leave to cool, then add the Framboise and lemon juice.

Meanwhile brush the inside of the moulds with non-scented oil, I use light groundnut or sunflower oil.

'Sponge' the gelatine in the 3 tablespoons of water, then place the bowl in a pan of simmering water until the gelatine has completely dissolved.

Remove the mint leaves from the syrup, then pour the syrup on to the gelatine. Mix well. Add the raspberries and stir gently. Fill immediately into the oiled moulds, smoothing them over the top so they will not be wobbly when you later unmould them on to a plate. Put them into the refrigerator and leave to set for 3–4 hours or overnight.

Meanwhile make the Mint Cream. Crush the mint leaves to a paste in a pestle and mortar with the lemon juice. Add the cream and stir – the lemon juice will thicken the cream. If the cream becomes too thick, add a little water.

To serve: spread a little Mint Cream on a chilled plate, unmould a raspberry jelly and place in the centre. Arrange five mint leaves on the mint cream around the jelly and decorate with a few perfect raspberries. Repeat with the other jellies. Serve chilled.

Poached Plums with Mascarpone Cheese

SERVES 4

400g (14oz) sugar
450ml (³/₄ pint) water
900g (2lb) fresh plums (Victoria, Opal or those dark Italian plums that come into the shops in autumn)
Mascarpone cheese
Caster sugar to taste

Poach the plums whole – they will taste better, but quite apart from that you will have the fun of playing 'He loves me – he loves me not!' You could just fix it by making sure you take an uneven number! The poached plums keep very well in a refrigerator and are delicious for breakfast – without the Mascarpone.

Put the sugar and water into a saucepan and bring to the boil slowly. Tip in the plums, cover the saucepan and poach until they begin to burst. Turn into a bowl and serve warm with some sweetened Mascarpone cheese melting over the top. Divine.

Julia Wight's Quince Paste

Quinces
Sugar

YOU WILL NEED
2 x 23 x 30cm (9 x 12in) approx. Swiss
roll tins
A mouli-légume

Quince is the most beautiful fruit and so wonderfully fragrant. If you bring a bowlful into the kitchen they will perfume the whole house. By the time I can finally bear to cook my quinces they are often too old to use. My friend Julia Wight, whose food I adore, makes this quince paste every year and her friends vie for her affections in order to secure a gift of it!

This paste is absolutely delicious served with a spoonful of soft goat's cheese and a leaf of sweet cicely or rose geranium. Julia also loves quince paste with Stilton or Cashel Blue cheese.

Preheat the oven to 100°C/200°F/gas mark 1/4.

With a cloth rub the down off the skins of as many quinces as you can pack into a large earthenware jar. Do not add any water. Cover the pot and place in a low oven for about 4 hours until the fruit is easily pierced with a skewer. Quarter the fruit, remove the core and any blemishes and put the pieces through a mouli-légume, using the biggest disc. (If you do not have one, buy one!)

Weigh the quince pulp and add three parts of sugar to every four parts of pulp. Cook the mixture in a preserving pan over a medium heat, and stir continuously with a wooden spatula until the mixture becomes rich in colour and it stops running together again when the spatula is drawn through the mixture.

Line 2 Swiss roll tins with baking parchment, fill with the paste and leave overnight to get quite cold.

The following day, dry the tins of paste out in a low oven (100°C/200°F/gas mark 1/4) for about 4 hours until it is quite firm. Check it is ready by lifting a corner of the paste: it should be solid all the way through. When the paste has cooled, cut in four strips, wrap in baking parchment and store in an airtight container. It will keep for about 4 months, but is best eaten when freshly made, cut into 2.5cm (1in) squares as a sweetmeat.

Sloe or Damson Gin

Sloes are very tart little berries that are like tiny purple plums in appearance; they grow on prickly bushes on the top of stone walls and are also found in the hedgerows around our farm. They are in season in September and October. Damsons, sometimes called bullaces, also autumn fruits, are less tart and plump than sloes and can be interchanged in this recipe.

MAKES 1.4 LITRES (2½ PINTS)

600ml (1 pint) measure of sloes or damsons
350g (12oz) white sugar
1.2 litres (2 pints) gin or poteen

On our 12-week course we take the students out to pick damsons and sloes. They are always disappointed that the sloe gin is only made as a demonstration! I make a lot of Sloe Gin and give it away as Christmas presents. It is lethal as it slips down so easily! You can also sweeten it and freeze it as a granita.

Wash and dry the sloes or damsons. Prick each one in several places – we use a clean darning needle. It sounds tedious, but can be enjoyable if you make yourself a cup of coffee, psyche yourself up, and turn your thoughts to Christmas, by which time your sloe or damson gin will taste wonderful and make great gifts.

Put the prepared fruit into a sterilized glass Kilner jar or a wide-necked bottle. Cover with the sugar and gin and seal tightly. Shake the container every other day to start with and then every now and then for 3–4 months, by which time it will be ready to strain and bottle. It will improve with keeping, so try to resist drinking it for another few months.

Winter

The shell house looks stunning with the thin winter light filtering through the diamond shaped panes of the Gothic windows. Timmy fought long and hard to dissuade me from this folly but, in the end, it was built and now he adores it.

Perhaps it is because I was reared far from the sea that I have always been enchanted by sea shells. I'd been collecting them in a haphazard way for years and they were piling up everywhere. Timmy lives in perpetual fear of my next crazy idea and, as the collection of shells got larger and larger, he knew I would eventually build them into something. Then I came across an article in one of our old gardening books about a shell grotto, mysterious and fantastical, and I was inspired to create something similar.

Left and above: the octagonal shellhouse, at the end of the herbacious borders, is a memorable feature adjacent to the yew maze, planted in 1996. It is truly one of my 'follies' and stands as a monument to Timmy's patience and understanding. It was built to house Blot Kerr Wilson's amazing displays of my shell collection which had been piling up for years. Our initials and those of the children, together with the date it was built, are included in the pattern of the shells. We bought the Gothic-style windows (above) from an architectural salvage yard.

'Fate is great': by sheer chance I was leafing through *Gardens Illustrated* magazine and there, just when I needed it, was an article about a wild and wonderful girl called Blot Kerr Wilson, who adored shells and had decorated every available surface in her semi-detached home with shells, including the loo, bathroom, corridor... I telephoned her instantly – no reply, just an answering machine and I left a breathless message: 'Call me back. If a man answers, put the phone down.'

Blot came, we schemed and she started work. Very soon I knew that she was going to create a masterpiece, much, much more artistic than I would ever have been able to make it, had I had the time. It took five months to complete the shell house. Blot's friends, Ben and Purdy, came to help and in the end it was completed on 26th October 1995, one day before our 25th wedding anniversary. It now stands as a monument to Timmy's patience in putting up with me all these years!

In winter, we get super, freshly dug parsnips which Haulie brings in old sacks, still covered with clay. I explain to the students the importance of buying root vegetables with the clay on; they keep better and taste better. Then there are the turnips, early Brussels sprouts, winter carrots and leeks, Chinese and Jerusalem artichokes, plenty to comfort and nourish. The swede turnips are particularly sweet, sprinkled with caramelized onions and freshly chopped parsley – even the most ardent turnip snobs will melt!

Mr Fitzsimmons brings us his gorgeous free-range chickens and Nora Aherne rears us tasty ducks, geese and turkeys, all raised naturally of course. You can imagine how many we get through with forty-plus students, and we have a huge turkey for our Christmas feast. Christmas is always a big family gathering – maybe thirty or more of us congregate with Myrtle and Ivan at Ballymaloe House. The Christmas meal is a grand affair: oysters and champagne around the fire; roast turkey with buttery herb stuffing, Brussels sprouts, cranberry sauce and our favourite bread sauce; then moist plum pudding and brandy butter. We pile up the presents under the tree and, after lunch is finished, the youngest child picks a present and gives it to Granda, the eldest, then everybody gets one and so the process goes on and on – until we're all ready for tea. We play country house games the children love to play, like sardines and post office. Eileen decorates our conservatory at Kinoith with lots of holly and pine cones, and we hand-string great rafts of chillies, nuts and citrus fruit.

Lemons, kumquats and oranges ripen in the conservatory. The Meyer lemons are exquisite and, occasionally, I'll pick one for a very special friend. It's a serious bit of one upmanship to have a home-grown lemon for a gin and tonic!

Just before Christmas, students from our second three-month course prepare to leave. At first they had to job-hunt for themselves. Now the School is better recognized through the grand work of our talented ex-students, we are approached by people from all over the world. I'm a member of the International Association of Culinary Professionals (the IACP) and they have a vast directory of contacts. If someone needs a chef in Sri Lanka or in Dublin they'll contact us. If a student in South Africa hears of an opportunity, they will fax back to the School. One boy was made Chalet Boy of the Year a couple of years ago, and we were thrilled when our daughter Lydia was chosen as Chalet Girl of the Year by Simply Ski. At the outset we had to ask potential employers to consider our students, who'd have to pay their fares to attend an interview; now companies fly out to visit us. Very gratifying.

Winter in the garden is a period of quiet, when we scan the seed catalogues and decide what we'd like to plant for the coming season. Not much happens around the farm. We tidy up, and clean out the potting shed. If it's mild, we propagate, plants are divided in the herbaceous border, and pruning has to be done. If we get snow, it's a huge excitement for a couple of days; if we get snow for a week the whole place nearly comes to a standstill. I've now got a wood-burning stove in the School, and one for our own winter hearth, too.

Above: in the lean winter months the rose bower provides a strong architectural feature in the garden when there is little in flower.

Left: it is a joy to watch the ducks on the pond at the end of Lydia's garden.

Below: we decorate the Bay tree with chillies to cheer us up in the winter.

In the flower garden, the winter sweet and the mahonia in the part we call the pleasure garden, near the potting shed, smell intoxicatingly delicious, as does the *Daphne odorata* by the garden gate. Under the office and the larder windows in front of the School there are winter-flowering rhododendrons which burst into flower each year, rewarding me when little else is in flower. The crop from our vegetable garden is reduced to sprouting broccoli and kale, still producing abundantly throughout January, and then we have lots of lambs lettuce and mysticana to liven up our winter salads.

As the New Year is ushered in, I start to think about our plans for the coming months. There's time to try out new ideas at home in my own kitchen, and to develop themes for new courses to run at the School. I will always want to expand the range of courses we offer. Of course there are some of the old favourites but it is important to be able to put in new ones and whatever takes my fancy that particular year.

Carrot and Cumin Soup

3 teaspoons whole cumin seeds
40g (1¹/₂oz) butter
560g (1¹/₄lb) Irish carrots, chopped
115g (4oz) onion, chopped
130g (5oz) potatoes, chopped
Salt, freshly ground black pepper and sugar
1.2litres (2 pints) Home-made Chicken Stock (see page 184)
65ml (2¹/₂fl oz) creamy milk (optional)

GARNISH
A little whipped cream or yoghurt
Freshly roasted and ground cumin
Coriander leaves

In our area of Ireland, acres and acres of carrots are grown. Piles of them heaped up by the side of the road are a common sight in autumn. This gutsy winter soup tastes great either hot or cold. Don't hesitate to put in a good pinch of sugar – it brings up the flavour.

Heat the cumin seeds in a frying pan, just for a minute or two until they smell rich and spicy. Grind in a pestle and mortar or a spice grinder. Melt the butter in a medium-sized saucepan. When it foams, add the chopped vegetables and the cumin seeds. Season with salt, pepper and sugar. Cover with a butter paper and a tight-fitting lid. Allow to sweat gently on a low heat for about 10 minutes or until the vegetables have softened slightly. Remove the lid. Add the stock, increase the heat and boil until the vegetables are soft.

Pour the lot into a liquidizer and purée until smooth. Taste and adjust the seasoning. Add a little creamy milk if necessary.

To serve: garnish each portion with a blob of whipped cream or yoghurt, sprinkle with a little ground cumin and top with a coriander leaf.

Spiced Chick-pea Soup

225g (8oz) chick-peas, soaked overnight in plenty of cold water
1.4 litres (2¹/₂ pints) Home-made Chicken or Vegetable Stock (see pages 184–5)
2–3 teaspoons coriander seeds
2–3 teaspoons cumin seeds
55g (2oz) butter
175g (6oz) onion, finely chopped
5 large cloves garlic, peeled and finely chopped
1–2 small red chillies, halved, deseeded and chopped
¹/₂ teaspoon ground turmeric
90ml (3fl oz) cream
Salt and freshly ground black pepper

GARNISH
Crème fraîche, coriander leaves

A winter soup to warm and fill you!

Drain the chick-peas and put them into a saucepan. Cover with the chicken or vegetable stock and bring to the boil. Cover and simmer gently for 45–60 minutes, or until the chick-peas are soft and tender.

Meanwhile, dry roast the coriander and cumin seeds in a frying pan on medium heat for 2–3 minutes, then crush in a pestle and mortar or spice grinder.

Melt the butter in a saucepan. Add the chopped onion, the crushed seeds, crushed garlic and chopped chilli. Cook gently for 4–5 minutes, add the turmeric, stir and cook for 1–2 minutes. Take the pan off the heat when the chick-peas are soft and tender. Mix everything together.

Liquidize the chick-peas with the cooking liquid and cream. Put back in a saucepan and simmer for 10–20 minutes. If the soup is a little too thick, thin down with extra stock.

Serve in hot soup bowls with a little crème fraîche. Sprinkle with fresh coriander leaves and serve.

Winter Vegetable and Bean Soup with Spicy Sausage

SERVES 8–9

225g (8oz) rindless streaky bacon, cut into 5mm (^{1}/4in) lardons
2 tablespoons olive oil
225g (8oz) onions, chopped
300g (10oz) carrots, cut into 5mm (^{1}/4in) dice
215g (7^1/2oz) celery, cut into 5mm (^{1}/4in) dice
125g (4^1/2oz) parsnips, cut into 5mm (^{1}/4in) dice
200g (7oz) white part of leeks, cut into 5mm (^{1}/4in) slices
1 Kabanossi or Kabonos sausage, cut into 3mm (^{1}/8in) thin slices
1 x 400g (14oz) tin of tomatoes, chopped
225g (8oz) haricot beans, cooked
Salt, freshly ground black pepper and sugar
1.7 litres (3 pints) Home-made Chicken Stock (see page 184)

GARNISH
2 tablespoons freshly chopped parsley

This comforting soup makes good use of all the winter produce from the vegetable garden and we make huge pots of it as a starter – and I usually keep some in the freezer. Kabanossi is a thin sausage now widely available; it gives the soup a gutsy, slightly smoky flavour which, although satisfying, is by no means essential.

Blanch the bacon lardons, refresh and dry well. Put the olive oil in a saucepan, add the bacon and sauté over a medium heat until it becomes crisp and golden. Add the chopped onions, carrots and celery. Cover and sweat for 5 minutes, next add the diced parsnip and finely sliced leeks. Cover and sweat for a further 5 minutes. Add the sliced sausage and chopped tomatoes with the beans to the rest of the vegetables. Season with salt, pepper and sugar. Add the chicken stock and continue to cook until all the vegetables are tender, about 20 minutes. Taste and correct the seasoning.

To serve, sprinkle with the chopped parsley and serve with lots of crusty brown bread.

Thai Chicken, Galingale and Coriander Soup

SERVES 8

900ml (32fl oz) Home-made Chicken Stock
(see page 184)
4 kaffir lime leaves
5cm (2in) piece of galingale, or 2.5cm (1in)
piece of ginger, peeled and sliced
4 tablespoons fish sauce (the Squid brand
is a good one)
6 tablespoons freshly squeezed lemon juice
225g (8oz) chicken breast, finely sliced
230ml (8fl oz) coconut milk (the Chaokoh
brand is the best)
2–3 red Thai chillies
About 5 tablespoons fresh coriander leaves

A particularly delicious example of how fast and easy a Thai soup can be.

Put the chicken stock, lime leaves, galingale (or ginger), fish sauce and lemon juice into a saucepan. Bring to the boil stirring all the time. Add the chicken and coconut milk. Continue to cook over a high heat until the chicken is just cooked, about 1–2 minutes.

Crush the chillies with a knife or Chinese chopper and add to the soup with some coriander leaves just a few seconds before ladling it into hot bowls. Serve immediately.

A Plate of Smoked Fish with Horseradish Mayonnaise and Sweet Dill Mayonnaise

SERVES 4

A selection of smoked fish –
salmon, mackerel, trout, smoked eel,
tuna, hake and sprats

ACCOMPANIMENT
Horseradish Mayonnaise (see page 186)
Sweet Dill Mayonnaise (see page 187)

GARNISH
Segments of lemon
Sprigs of watercress or rocket leaves

Occasionally we serve just three different types of smoked fish – for example salmon, mussels and trout – on tiny rounds of brown yeast bread, topped with a little frill of fresh lollo rosso. A small blob of Cucumber Pickle (see page 187) goes with Bill Casey's smoked salmon, homemade Sweet Dill Mayonnaise is delicious with Frank Hederman's marinated smoked mussels, and Horseradish Mayonnaise with a little sprig of watercress complements the pink smoked trout or herring from Sally Barnes – these delicious morsels make a perfect light starter.

Thinly slice the salmon down on to the skin; allow one slice per person. Cut the mackerel into diamond-shaped pieces. Divide the trout into large flakes. Skin and slice the eel. Slice the tuna and the hake thinly.

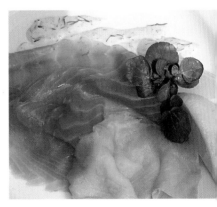

To serve, choose four large plates and drizzle each one with Sweet Dill Mayonnaise. Divide the smoked fish between the plates. Put a blob of Horseradish Mayonnaise on each plate. Garnish with a lemon wedge and sprigs of watercress or rocket leaves.

Soused Herring, Cucumber Pickle and Sweet Dill Mayonnaise

SERVES 16 AS A STARTER
(8 AS A MAIN COURSE)

8 herrings
1 onion, thinly sliced
1 teaspoon whole black peppercorns
6 whole cloves
1 teaspoon salt
1 teaspoon sugar
300ml (1/2 pint) white wine vinegar
1 bay leaf

Cucumber Pickle (see page 187)
Sweet Dill Mayonnaise (see page 187)

We get masses of herring brought into Ballycotton, although the season for them is short. This one of the many ways in which we use them.

Preheat the oven to 140°C/270°F/gas mark 1.

Gut, wash and fillet the herrings, making sure there are no bones – a tall order with herring, but do your best. Roll up the fillets skin-side out and pack tightly into a cast-iron casserole. Sprinkle over the onion, peppercorns, cloves, salt, sugar, vinegar and bay leaf. Bring to the boil on top of the cooker and then pop into the preheated oven for 30–45 minutes. Allow to get quite cold. Soused herring will keep for 7–10 days in the refrigerator.

To serve: put one or two fillets of soused herring on a plate, surround with three little mounds of Cucumber Pickle, and zigzag with Sweet Dill Mayonnaise. Fresh crusty bread is a must!

151

Seared Beef Salad with Crispy Onions and Horseradish Mayonnaise

SERVES 6

Selection of salad leaves

DRESSING
4 tablespoons extra virgin olive oil
1 tablespoon white wine vinegar
1/4 teaspoon Lakeshore grainy mustard
1 teaspoon freshly chopped herbs (thyme, parsley and tarragon would be good)
Salt and freshly ground pepper

CRISPY ONIONS
1 large onion
Milk
Seasoned flour
Good quality oil or beef dripping for deep frying

6–18 x 5mm (1/4in) thick slices of Irish beef fillet – use 1 slice per person from the mid fillet or 3 slices from the tapered end
Salt and freshly ground black pepper
Olive oil

GARNISH
Horseradish Mayonnaise (see page 186)
A few fresh rocket leaves
Freshly cracked black pepper

This is a quick and easy salad which can be also be served as a main course. Freshly grated horseradish gives the sauce a good kick, and if you want it to be pungent just add more! If you cannot buy it in your local shops it is well worth growing your own, but watch it carefully as it spreads like mad. Strips of roast red pepper and crumbled blue cheese are also a good alternative topping.

Wash and dry the salad leaves. Make the dressing by whisking all the ingredients together in a bowl. Season well.

Prepare and cook the crispy onions. Slice the onion horizontally into 5mm (1/4in) rings. Separate the rings and cover with the milk until needed. Just before serving, heat the oil to 180°C (350°F). Toss the rings a few at a time lightly in well-seasoned flour. Deep-fry until golden, drain on kitchen paper and keep hot.

Heat a grill pan on a high heat. Season the beef on both sides with salt and pepper and a drizzle of olive oil. Sear the beef on the hot grill pan, first in one direction and then the other to give a criss-cross effect. Toss the salad leaves in just enough dressing to make the leaves glisten.

Just before serving divide the salad between each of the warm plates, piling the leaves up in the centre. Arrange the seared beef around the leaves. Dribble a little Horseradish Mayonnaise over each slice of beef. Put a clump of hot crispy onions on top of the salad. Serve immediately with a rocket leaf or two on each plate and a little sprinkling of freshly cracked pepper.

Cloyne Black Pudding with Glazed Apples and Grainy Mustard Sauce

SERVES 4

GLAZED APPLES
2 dessert apples (Worcester Pearmain, Cox's or Golden Delicious)
Juice of $^1/_4$ –$^1/_2$ lemon
1 tablespoon caster sugar
25g (1oz) butter

Grainy Mustard Sauce (see page 182)

Butter
3–4 x 1cm ($^1/_2$in) slices of black pudding per person (we use Kirrane's from Cloyne, or Clonakilty Black Pudding)

GARNISH
Flat-leaf parsley

Black and white puddings are traditional Irish breakfast food. My brother Rory created this combination. In Ireland we have a national competition for the best black pudding and, as a happy consequence, regional differences are preserved and producers vie to keep up their very high standards. We get our pudding from Kirrane's in Cloyne, which is just 2 miles from us, or Clonakilty Black Pudding, which may be bought in the UK and the US. If you cannot find it, use the French boudin noir.

Peel, core and cut the apples neatly into 5mm ($^1/_4$in) slices. Melt the butter in a sauté pan and when it foams, add the apple slices and coat gently in the butter. Add the sugar and lemon juice. Cook slowly for about 5 minutes, or until the apples are glazed in a shiny syrup. Keep warm.

Next make the Mustard Sauce. Melt a little butter in a frying pan and cook the slices of black pudding on both sides on a medium heat until heated through. Don't let the slices get too crusty on the outside.

To serve: divide the warm apple slices between four hot plates. Arrange the slices of black pudding on the apples and spoon a little Mustard Sauce carefully over the top. Garnish each with a sprig of flat parsley and serve immediately.

Fresh Cheese Ravioli with Parsley Pesto and Tomato Fondue

SERVES 8

PASTA – MAKES 585G (1LB 5OZ)
400g (14oz) plain white flour
1 teaspoon salt (optional)
3–4 eggs, preferably free-range

225g (8oz) Home-made Cottage Cheese
(see page 94) or soft goat's cheese
85g (3oz) Parmesan (Parmigiano
Reggiano) cheese, freshly grated
2 tablespoons parsley, finely chopped
Salt and freshly ground black pepper
Grated nutmeg

Tomato Fondue (see page 182)
250ml (8fl oz) cream
3 tablespoons butter
85g (3oz) Parmesan cheese
Parsley Pesto (see page 186)

GARNISH
Flat-leaf parsley

Pasta machines, either hand-cranked or with an electric motor, are well worth buying if you make pasta on a regular basis. We serve these ravioli with all sorts of garnishes – roasted red pepper, char-grilled aubergines, buttered cabbage, black olives... The possibilities are unlimited.

First make the pasta. Sieve the flour into a bowl and add the salt if using. Whisk the eggs together, make a well in the centre of the flour and add in most of the egg. Mix into a dough with your hand, adding the remaining egg if you need it. The pasta should just come together but should not stick to your hand – if it does, add a little more flour. (If it is very much too wet, it is very difficult to get it right.) Knead for a few minutes until smooth and then rest on a plate covered with an upturned bowl for 1 hour to relax.

Divide the dough in half and roll out one piece at a time into a very thin sheet, keeping the other piece covered. You ought to be able to read the print on a matchbox through the pasta. A long thin rolling pin is a great advantage but you can manage perfectly well with an ordinary domestic rolling pin. Don't allow the pasta to dry: cover it with a tea towel while you make the filling.

Mix the cottage cheese with the freshly grated Parmesan and finely chopped parsley. Season well with salt, pepper and a little nutmeg.

To assemble, put a sheet of pasta on the work top and brush lightly with cold water. Put teaspoons of filling about 4cm (1½in) apart on the pasta. Lay another identical-sized sheet of pasta on top, seal the edges loosely and press out the air gently with the side of your hand. Cut into squares with a pastry wheel or stamp out rounds with a small glass or a fluted cutter.

The ravioli can be cooked immediately or refrigerated for a few hours. However, this delicate filling is perishable so the ravioli should be cooked on the same day. Bring 4.5 litres (8 pints) water to a fast rolling boil and add 2 tablespoons salt. Shoot in the ravioli and put the lid back on the saucepan until the water returns to the boil.

Meanwhile, heat the Tomato Fondue. Put the cream and butter into a wide sauté pan and allow to bubble for a minute. The ravioli will be cooked in about 5 minutes. Test, drain and add to the bubbling cream. Add the Parmesan cheese. Toss gently until the ravioli is nicely coated.

Serve with Tomato Fondue and a little Parsley Pesto and garnish with the flat-leaf parsley.

Gratin of Cod with Imokilly Cheddar and Mustard

SERVES 6

6 x 175g (6oz) pieces of cod
Salt and freshly ground black pepper
225g (8oz) Irish mature Cheddar cheese
1 tablespoon Dijon mustard
4 tablespoons cream

Piquant Beetroot (see page 168)

YOU WILL NEED
Ovenproof dish 20 x 25cm (8 x 10in),
buttered

This is one of the simplest and most delicious fish dishes we know. If cod is unavailable, haddock, hake or grey sea mullet are also great. We use Imokilly mature Cheddar cheese from our local creamery at Mogeely but you can use any good, well-flavoured mature Cheddar.

Preheat the oven to 180°C/350°F/gas mark 4.

Season the fish with salt and pepper. Arrange the fillets in a single layer in an ovenproof dish (it should be posh enough to bring to the table). Grate the cheese, mix with the mustard and cream and spread carefully over the fish. It can be prepared ahead and refrigerated at this point. Cook in the preheated oven for about 20 minutes or until the fish is cooked and the top is golden and bubbly. Flash under the grill if necessary.

Serve with hot Piquant Beetroot.

Salmon with Swiss Chard

SERVES 6

675g (1½lb) salmon fillet (get the thick centre of a large salmon and ask the fishmonger to remove the skin)
Salt and freshly ground black pepper
350g (12oz) Swiss chard or ruby chard
4 tablespoons olive oil
1 large onion, thinly sliced
A 4cm (1½in) cube of fresh ginger, peeled and cut into very thin slices, then into fine slivers (or use a slivery grater)
8 tinned plum tomatoes, chopped
1 teaspoon sugar
125ml (4fl oz) thick coconut milk (we use Chaokoh brand)

Madhur Jaffrey introduced me to this combination, which she discovered in the Philippines. It is a great recipe for a dinner party.

Remove any bones from the fish with tweezers. Cut the salmon fillet into six portions. Season the fish with salt and pepper and set aside while you prepare the chard. Swiss chard has a central stalk bordered by spinach-like leaves. Strip the leaf from the stalk. Cut the leafy section, crossways, into 5mm (¼in) wide strips. Set aside. Then slice the stalks crossways into 3mm (⅛in) wide strips.

Heat the oil in a very wide sauté pan or large frying pan on a medium heat. Add the onion, ginger and chard stems. Sauté, stirring occasionally, for about 5 minutes. Add the chopped tomatoes and the sugar and continue to sauté for another 4–5 minutes. Add the coconut milk and 350ml (12fl oz) of water and season well with salt and some pepper. Stir, bring to the boil and then simmer on a low heat for a minute. (The recipe can be prepared ahead up to this point.)

Just before serving, bring the sauce to simmering point again. Stir in the chard leaves and arrange the salmon pieces in a single layer over the top of the sauce. Spoon some of the liquid over the fish. Cover with a tight-fitting lid and simmer for 4–5 minutes, or until the salmon has just cooked through.

To serve, lift the fish and chard on to a hot serving dish. Spoon the sauce over the top of the fish and serve immediately.

Steak and Oyster Pie

SERVES 4–6

630g (1¹/₂lb) best quality beef, such as round steak, best chuck or thick rib steak

Salt and freshly ground black pepper

25g (1oz) butter

1 large onion, about 225g (8oz), chopped

1 tablespoon white flour

600ml (1 pint) Home-made Beef Stock (see page 185)

225g (8oz) sliced mushrooms

12 Gigas or Native Irish oysters

Roux, if necessary (see page 182)

275g (9oz) Puff Pastry (see page 183)

Egg wash

YOU WILL NEED

A 1.1litre (2 pint) pie dish

This may seem to be a modern combination but in fact it is an old classic which dates back to a time when oysters were ten a penny and were put in to bulk out the steak! Gigas oysters are less expensive than native oysters and are available the whole year round.

Cut the beef into 4cm (1¹/₂in) cubes, season with salt and pepper. Melt a little butter in a frying pan and seal the meat over a high heat. Move the meat to a plate, add the onions to the pan and cook for about 5–6 minutes. Remove the pan from the heat and stir in the flour. Return to the heat and cook for 1 minute. Blend in the stock, add the meat and bring to the boil. Transfer to a flameproof casserole, cover and simmer on a low heat for 1¹/₂–2 hours. Alternatively place in a preheated oven (160°C/325°F/gas mark 3) for 1¹/₂–2 hours.

Meanwhile, sauté the mushrooms in a frying pan in the remaining butter on a high heat. Season with salt and pepper, set aside. Open the oysters and put in a bowl with their juice. When the meat is tender, thicken the cooking juices slightly with roux if necessary. Add the mushrooms, oysters and their juice and taste for seasoning. Bring to the boil for 3 or 4 minutes. Allow to get cold and put into the pie dish.

Preheat the oven to 250°C/475°F/gas mark 9. Roll out the pastry to about 5mm (¹/₄in) thickness and cover the pie, flute the edges and garnish with pastry leaves. Brush with egg wash and cook in the preheated oven for 10 minutes, then reduce the temperature to 190°C/375°F/ gas mark 5 and cook for a further 15–20 minutes or until the pastry is puffed and golden.

Venison Stew with Potato and Parsnip Mash

SERVES 8

1.3kg (3lb) shoulder of venison, trimmed
Salt and freshly ground black pepper
Seasoned flour

MARINADE

300–330ml (10–11fl oz) full-bodied red wine
1 medium onion, sliced
3 tablespoons brandy
3 tablespoons olive oil
Salt and freshly cracked black pepper
A sprig of thyme, marjoram and a bay leaf

SAUCE

225g (8oz) fat streaky bacon, diced
2 tablespoons olive oil
2 large onions, chopped
2 large carrots, diced
1 large clove garlic, crushed
425ml (15fl oz) venison stock or Home-made
Chicken Stock (see page 184)
Bouquet garni
24 small (about 250g/9oz) fresh mushrooms,
preferably wild ones, sliced
Butter
Salt and freshly ground black pepper
Cream (optional)
Chopped parsley (optional)
Thyme leaves (optional)
Lemon juice (optional)

Our venison comes from the Ballinatray estate near Youghal. The sweet flavour of parsnips works well with venison.

Dice the venison and season well. Put in a bowl and add the marinade ingredients. Cover and refrigerate for 12–24 hours. Drain the meat well, pat it dry on kitchen paper and turn lightly in seasoned flour.

Preheat the oven to 150°C/300°F/gas mark 2.

Brown the cubes of streaky bacon for the sauce in the olive oil in a frying pan. Cook them slowly at first to render out the fat, then raise the heat to get them crispy on the outside. Transfer to a flameproof casserole.

Brown the venison in the sizzling fat and then add the onions, carrots and garlic, in batches, transferring each one to the casserole. Control the heat carefully or the fat will burn. Pour off any surplus fat, deglaze the pan with the marinade and pour the liquid over the venison. Heat up enough stock just to cover the meat and vegetables in the casserole and pour it over them. Add the bouquet garni, bring to a gentle simmer on top of the stove and transfer to the preheated oven. Cover tightly and continue to cook until the venison is tender and melting. Test after $1\frac{1}{2}$ hours, but it may take up to $2\frac{1}{2}$ hours.

For best results, we cook this casserole a day ahead and then reheat it the next. This improves the flavour and ensures the venison is tender.

Sauté the sliced mushrooms in a little butter. Season with salt and pepper and add to the stew. I sometimes add a little cream and some chopped parsley and thyme too. Finally taste the sauce: it may need seasoning and perhaps a squeeze of lemon juice. It often benefits from a pinch of sugar or a spoonful of redcurrant jelly (be careful not to use too much).

Serve with Potato and Parsnip Mash (see page 166).

Pheasant with Jerusalem Artichokes

Pheasant adore Jerusalem artichokes; most of the large estates in Ireland plant a special patch as a treat for them. It seemed logical to cook them together, and indeed it has turned out to be a very good marriage of flavours. Chicken or guinea-fowl may also be cooked in this manner.

SERVES 4

25g (1oz) butter
1 plump pheasant
900g (2lb) Jerusalem artichokes
Salt and freshly ground black pepper

GARNISH
Chopped parsley or sprigs of
flat-leaf parsley

Preheat the oven to 180°C/350°F/gas mark 4.

Smear a little butter on the breast of the pheasant and brown it in a flame-proof casserole over a gentle heat. Meanwhile, peel the artichokes and slice into 1cm (1/2in) pieces. Remove the pheasant from the casserole, add a little butter and toss the slices of Jerusalem artichoke in it. Season with salt and pepper and sprinkle maybe a tablespoon of water over the top. Then replace the pheasant, tucking it right down into the sliced artichokes so they come up around the sides of the bird. Cover with a butter wrapper and the lid of the casserole. Cook for 1–1 1/4 hours. Remove the pheasant as soon as it is cooked. Strain and degrease the cooking liquid if necessary (but usually there is virtually no fat on it). The juices of the pheasant will have flavoured the artichokes deliciously. Arrange the artichokes on a hot serving dish. Carve the pheasant into four portions and arrange on top. The artichokes always break up a little – that is their nature. Spoon some juices over the pheasant and artichokes.

Serve scattered with chopped parsley or flat-leaf parsley sprigs.

Roast Stuffed Duck with Beetroot

SERVES 4

Home-made Duck Stock (see page 185)

1 free-range duck (about 1.8kg/4lb)

SAGE AND ONION STUFFING
85g (3oz) onions, finely chopped
40g (1 1/2oz) butter
100g (3 1/2oz) soft white breadcrumbs
1 tablespoon sage, freshly chopped
Salt and freshly ground black pepper

Bramley Apple Sauce (see page 187)

Piquant Beetroot (see page 168)

Nora Ahearne rears us the most beautiful free-range ducks and geese – make enquiries in your area and if you find a treasure like Nora, someone willing to rear poultry of this quality for you, be prepared to pay a premium price for a bird – it will be worth every penny. Beetroot goes particularly well with roast goose and duck , and also with pork with crackling.

Singe off any remaining whiskers from the duck using a taper or hold the bird over the gas jet of the stove.

To make the stuffing, sweat the onions in the butter on a gentle heat for 5–10 minutes until soft but not coloured. Add the breadcrumbs and sage. Season with salt and pepper to taste. Unless you plan to cook the duck immediately, allow the stuffing to get cold.

Preheat the oven to 180°C/350°F/gas mark 4.

When the stuffing is quite cold, season the cavity of the duck and spoon in the stuffing. Roast in the preheated oven for about 1 1/2 hours.

Meanwhile make the Bramley Apple Sauce.

When the duck is cooked, remove to a serving dish and allow to rest while you make the gravy. Heat the stock. Degrease the cooking juices (keeping the duck fat for roast or sauté potatoes). Add the stock to the juices in the roasting pan, bring to the boil, taste and season if necessary. Strain the gravy into a sauce boat.

Serve the duck with warm apple sauce, beetroot and gravy.

Sweet-Sour Pork with Prunes, Raisins, Pine Kernels and Polenta

SERVES 8–10

MARINADE
6 juniper berries
10 black peppercorns
2 bay leaves
1/2 teaspoon thyme leaves
1 carrot, chopped
1 onion, chopped
1 stick celery, chopped
725ml (24fl oz) or more dry red wine
50ml (2fl oz) red wine vinegar

1.7kg (4lb) boneless shoulder or leg of pork, cubed
5 tablespoons olive oil
Sea salt
180ml (6fl oz) red wine vinegar
Freshly ground black pepper
36 prunes, soaked in water
55g (2oz) raisins, plumped in hot water
50g (1³/₄oz) pine nuts, toasted
2 tablespoons sugar
40g (1¹/₂oz) dark chocolate, grated

ACCOMPANIMENT
Polenta (see page 183)

Jo Bettoja, whose food I adore, served us this rich sweet-sour stew in her home in Rome. It is an old family recipe for wild boar that has been passed down through the generations. Timmy and I loved the rich gutsy flavour so she kindly shared her recipe with us.

Mix all the ingredients for the marinade together in a bowl. Add the cubes of pork and stir well. Cover and marinate for 48 hours in the refrigerator. Stir every now and then during this period.

Preheat the oven to 160°C/325°F/gas mark 3.

Drain the meat and reserve the marinade and the vegetables. Dry the meat on kitchen paper. Heat 4 tablespoons of the olive oil in a frying pan on a high heat. Brown the meat on all sides and then transfer the pieces to a casserole and season with salt. Add a little more oil to the pan and cook the marinated vegetables for 10–15 minutes or until the onion is soft. Add a few tablespoons of the marinade to prevent the vegetables from burning. Add to the casserole. Deglaze the pan with the reserved marinade plus 50ml (2fl oz) of the vinegar, bring to the boil and scrape into the casserole. Add 1/2 teaspoon freshly ground black pepper, cover the casserole and cook in the preheated oven until the meat is tender, about 1¹/₂ hours.

Remove the meat to a bowl and strain the sauce into a saucepan. Press the vegetables through the sieve to get the last of the juices. Add the prunes, raisins and pine nuts to the sauce.

In another small saucepan simmer the remaining red wine vinegar with 2 tablespoons sugar for 4 minutes, then add to the sauce with the chocolate and the meat. Bring to the boil slowly and simmer for 15 minutes. Taste and adjust the seasoning if necessary.

Serve with soft Polenta and follow with a good green salad.

Black-eyed Beans and Chick-pea Stew

This recipe is suitable for vegetarians and vegans. We make lots of this kind of combination stew. Of course. you can use canned beans if you are in a hurry, but they are more expensive.

SERVES 6

225g (8oz) dried black-eyed beans

225g (8oz) chick-peas

225g (8oz) fresh mushrooms

6 tablespoons sunflower or groundnut oil

1 teaspoon whole cumin seeds

2.5cm (1in) piece of cinnamon stick

140g (5oz) onions, chopped

4 cloves garlic, very finely chopped

400g (14oz) fresh or tinned tomatoes, peeled and chopped

2 teaspoons ground coriander seeds

1 teaspoon ground cumin seeds

$^1/_2$ teaspoon ground turmeric

Pinch of sugar

$^1/_4$ teaspoon cayenne pepper

1 good teaspoon salt (it needs it)

Freshly ground black pepper

3 tablespoons freshly chopped coriander (fresh parsley may be substituted though the flavour is not at all the same)

1 tablespoon chopped fresh mint

Soak the beans and chick-peas separately in plenty of cold water overnight. The next day boil the pulses separately and rapidly for 10 minutes to remove the toxins. Drain, cover again with fresh water and simmer for 30–45 minutes or until just cooked.

Cut the mushrooms into 3mm ($^1/_8$in) thick slices. Heat the oil in a sauté pan over a medium-high flame. When hot, put in the whole cumin seeds and the cinnamon stick. Let them sizzle for 5–6 seconds. Now put in the onions and garlic. Stir and fry until the onions are just beginning to colour at the edge. Put in the mushrooms, stir and fry until they wilt. Now put in the tomatoes, ground coriander, ground cumin, turmeric, sugar and cayenne. Stir and cook for a minute. Cover the pan, and let this mixture cook on a gentle heat in its own juices for 10 minutes. Turn off the heat under the pan.

Drain the beans and the chick-peas, reserving the cooking liquid from each pan. Add to the mushroom base mixture and add salt and pepper, 2 tablespoons of the fresh coriander and 150ml ($^1/_4$ pint) of both the bean and the chick-pea cooking liquids. Bring the stew to the boil again. Reduce the heat and simmer for 10–20 minutes or until the beans and chick-peas are tender, stirring occasionally. Remove the cinnamon stick before serving.

Sprinkle with the remaining chopped coriander and the mint and serve with rice and a good green salad.

Tagine of Lamb with Preserved Lemons

SERVES 6

TAGINE

1.35kg (3lb) boned shoulder of lamb
1/2 tablespoon ground cinnamon
1 teaspoon ground ginger
1 teaspoon freshly ground black pepper
Generous pinch of saffron

55g (2oz) unsalted butter
2 onions, chopped
2 cloves garlic, finely chopped
Salt
175g (6oz) raisins, soaked in water and drained
2 tablespoons honey
3 tablespoons chopped coriander

1 Moroccan Preserved Lemon (see page 166)
55g (2oz) flaked almonds
1 tablespoons oil

The word 'tagine' refers to the distinctive earthenware cooking pot of Morocco and to the stew-like dishes cooked in it. These can be based on meat, fish or vegetables. I lugged my precious tagine, and its brazier, all the way from Marrakesh. Without question it is the most expensive tagine in the whole of Ireland, because although I got a bargain in the Medina, I had to pay excess baggage at the airport and the Moroccans would not settle for my left-over dirham – they wanted sterling or dollars and would not part with the tagine until they got them!

Trim the lamb, discarding the excess fat. Cut into 4cm (1 1/2in) cubes. Mix the cinnamon, ginger, pepper and saffron with 4 tablespoons water. Toss the lamb in this mixture. If you have time, marinate it for up to 24 hours.

Melt the butter in a wide pan. Add the lamb, onions, garlic, salt and just enough water to cover. Bring up to the boil, cover and reduce the heat to give a gentle simmer. Cook for about 1 hour, turning the lamb occasionally until the meat is meltingly tender. Then add the raisins, honey and half the coriander. Continue simmering, with the pan uncovered, for a further 30 minutes or so, until the sauce is thick and unctuous. Taste and adjust the seasoning.

While the tagine is cooking, scoop the flesh out of a Preserved Lemon (see page 166) and discard. Chop up the peel. Fry the almonds and the lemon peel in the oil until golden brown. Drain on kitchen paper. Sprinkle the almonds and remaining coriander over the lamb just before serving.

Roast Woodcock with Sweet Geranium Jelly

SERVES 4

4 woodcock

Pork caul fat or streaky bacon

55g (2oz) melted butter

Salt and freshly ground black pepper

4 croutons large enough for the birds

Butter

1 tablespoon brandy (optional)

GARNISH

Sprigs of watercress or a small bouquet of fresh herbs

Sweet Geranium Jelly (see page 188)

Woodcock and snipe are highly regarded not only for their delicious flesh but also for their innards – with the exception of the gizzard, which is removed before the birds are roasted. Pluck them carefully, head and all, because woodcock or snipe are traditionally served trussed with their own long beak. They are best hung for 4–5 days.

Preheat the oven to 230°C/450°F/gas mark 8.

Remove the gizzard from each bird by making a small incision in the thin skin of the abdomen, slightly to the right of the centre, near the vent. Locate the gizzard with a skewer or trussing needle – this is not as difficult as it sounds – it will feel like a hard lump. Remove and detach from the innards, which should remain in the bird.

Brush the birds with melted butter and season with salt and pepper. Wrap in pork caul or streaky bacon and secure with cotton thread or string.

Toast 4 slices of bread and butter one side. Put the toast buttered side down on a baking tray, put the woodcock on top and roast in the pre-heated oven for 18–22 minutes depending on size. They are usually cooked when the caul or bacon is crispy. A tablespoon of brandy may be added to the juices in the roasting tin: season with salt and pepper, warm through but do not boil.

To serve, arrange the croutons on a hot serving dish, spoon the sauce over and sit the birds on top. Garnish with sprigs of watercress or a little bouquet of fresh herbs. Serve with Sweet Geranium Jelly.

Swede Turnips with Caramelized Onions

SERVES ABOUT 6

900g (2lb) swede turnips
Salt and lots of freshly ground black
pepper
55–115g (2–4oz) butter or 55g (2oz) butter
and 80–125ml (3–4fl oz) cream

CARAMELIZED ONIONS
450g (1lb) onions, thinly sliced
2–3 tablespoons olive oil

GARNISH
Flat-leaf parsley, finely snipped

Swede turnips are sweetest after they have had a touch of frost; they are unquestionably one of the most underrated of all vegetables.

Peel the turnips generously to remove the thick outside skin. Cut into 2cm (³/₄in) cubes. Cover with fresh water. Add a good pinch of salt, bring to the boil and cook until soft.

Meanwhile make the caramelized onions. Heat the olive oil in a heavy saucepan. Toss in the onions and cook on a low heat for whatever length of time it takes for them to soften and caramelize to a golden brown, about 30–45 minutes. Remember to stir occasionally so they brown evenly. If you cannot be bothered to cook them long and slowly like this, put 1–1¹/₂ table-spoons of olive oil or mixed olive and sunflower oil into a frying pan. Heat to hot but not smoking. Fry a few thinly sliced onion rings at a time, drain in a wire sieve over a stainless steel bowl and then dry on kitchen paper. Continue until all the onions are cooked – faster but actually more labour-intensive. Save the onion-flavoured oil for sauté potatoes or crostini.

Strain off the excess water, mash the turnips well and beat in the butter and cream if using. Taste and season with lots of freshly ground pepper and more salt if necessary.

Sprinkle the caramelized onions over the top. Garnish with the parsley and serve piping hot.

Green Broccoli, Calabrese or Romanesco

SERVES 4

450g (1lb) calabrese or romanesco
1¹/₂ teaspoons salt
600ml (1 pint) water
Lots of freshly ground black pepper
15–30g (¹/₂–1oz) butter (optional)

The secret of real flavour in broccoli, calabrese and romanesco, as in many other green vegetables, is not just freshness; they need to be cooked in well-salted water. If you grow your own, cut out the central head but leave the plant intact; very soon you will have lots of smaller florets. WIth broccoli and calabrese don't discard the stalks: peel them and cook them. The grated stalk is also very good in a broccoli slaw.

Peel the stems of broccoli, calabrese or romanesco with a knife or potato peeler. Cut off the stalk close to the head into 1cm (¹/₂in) pieces. If the heads are large, divide the florets into small clusters. Add the salt to the water and bring to a fast boil. Add the stalks first and then the florets, and cook, uncovered, at a rolling boil for 5–6 minutes. Drain off the water while the broccoli still has a bite. Broccoli can be blanched and refreshed earlier in the day and then reheated in a saucepan of boiling salted water just before serving. Taste, season with pepper and serve immediately. Better still, melt a little butter in a saucepan until it foams, toss the broccoli gently in it, season to taste and serve immediately.

Curly Kale and its Cousins

SERVES ABOUT 4

450g (1lb) curly kale – about
300g (10oz) destalked
Salt, freshly ground black pepper
Nutmeg, grated (optional)
55g (2oz) butter
125ml (4fl oz) cream

Much as I love the winter root vegetables – parsnip, celeriac, swede turnips and so on – I also long for the clean sharp taste of greens in the late autumn and winter. Kale and the sprouting broccolis satisfy this need deliciously and, in the case of kale, most decoratively. We grow several different varieties apart from curly kale. Some of the leaves are serrated, others crinkly, others almost feathery; they come in most beautiful shades, from greeny grey to blue, green, deep purple, cream and yellow. Red Russian kale is one of our favourites, I can hardly bear to pick the deeply serrated leaves which look so beautiful in the winter garden covered with frost or in the early morning when the sun shines on the droplets of dew caught on the leaves – the tussle between the cook and gardener in me is at its most acute.

Put 3.4 litres (6 pints) of water and 3 teaspoons salt in a large saucepan and bring to the boil. Add the curly kale and boil uncovered on a high heat until tender: this can vary from 5–10 minutes depending on the texture. Drain off the water, purée in a food processor, return to the saucepan, season with salt, freshly ground pepper and a little nutmeg if you fancy. Add a nice lump of butter and some cream, bubble and taste. Serve hot.

Moroccan Preserved Lemons

5 lemons
55g (2oz) salt (pure dairy salt
– i.e. without additives)
Extra freshly squeezed lemon juice from
about 3–4 lemons

Preserved lemons are one of those initial 'yuk' tastes that later become addictive. Nothing else provides the authentic taste of Morocco in quite the same way. Add the lemon peel to tagines, fish stews, and soups – as well as salad dressing.

Wash the lemons thoroughly and quarter them from the top to within 1cm (1/2in) of the base. Sprinkle some salt on the flesh, then close and reshape the fruit. Put 2 tablespoons of salt in the bottom of a sterilized preserving jar. Pack in the lemons, pressing them down gently. Cover the fruit with the extra lemon juice and fill the jar to the top with boiling water.

Seal the jar and leave the lemons to mature for 30 days before using. They will keep for up to a year.

Potato and Parsnip Mash

SERVES ABOUT 8

450kg (1lb) 'old' potatoes, such as Golden
Wonder or Kerr's Pink
Salt and freshly ground black pepper
1.25kg (2½lb) parsnips
About 300–350ml (10–12fl oz) creamy milk
About 55g (2oz) butter

GARNISH
2 tablespoons chopped parsley

This is wonderful with Venison Stew (see page 158), as the slightly sweet taste and soft texture balance the meat perfectly.

Scrub the potatoes. Put them into a saucepan of cold water, add a good pinch of salt and bring to the boil. When the potatoes are about half-cooked (about 15 minutes for 'old' potatoes), strain off two-thirds of the water, replace the lid on the saucepan, put on a gentle heat and let the potatoes steam until they are cooked.

Peel the parsnips and cut into chunks. Cook in boiling, salted water until tender, then drain and mash. Keep warm.

When the potatoes are just cooked, put the milk in a saucepan and bring to the boil. Pull the peel off the potatoes, mash quickly while they are still warm and beat in enough boiling milk to make a fluffy mash. (If you have a large quantity, put the potatoes in the bowl of a food mixer and beat.) Then add the mashed parsnip with the butter. Taste for seasoning. Serve immediately or reheat later in a preheated oven at 180°C/350°F/gas mark 4 for about 20–25 minutes.

Serve in a hot dish with a scattering of parsley on top or, if you like, piled high with Parsnip Crisps (see page 127).

Winter Green Salad with Herb Vinaigrette Dressing

WINTER VINAIGRETTE
6 tablespoons extra virgin olive oil
2 tablespoons red wine vinegar
$1/2$ teaspoon Irish honey
1 teaspoon grainy mustard
Small clove garlic, crushed
2 tablespoons freshly chopped mixed herbs (parsley, chives, mint, watercress, thyme)
Salt and freshly ground black pepper

For this salad, use a selection of winter lettuces and salad leaves, e.g. butter-head, iceberg, radicchio, endive, chicory, watercress, buckler leaf , sorrel, rocket leaves, mysticana and winter purslane. The tips of purple sprouting broccoli are also delicious and, if you feel like something more robust, include some finely shredded Savoy cabbage and maybe a few shreds of red cabbage too.

Wash and dry the lettuces and salad leaves and tear into bite-sized pieces. Keep the smaller leaves such as purslane, rocket, buckler leaf and sorrel whole. Put all the leaves into a deep salad bowl, add the shredded cabbage and toss it all together.

To make the vinaigrette, put all the ingredients into a screw-topped jar, adding salt and pepper to taste. Shake well to emulsify the dressing before use; otherwise, whizz together all the ingredients in a food processor or liquidizer for a few seconds.

Just before serving, add a little vinaigrette and toss until the salad leaves are just glistening.

Celeriac and Apple Purée

450g (1lb) celeriac – weight after peeling
1 litre (1³/₄ pints) milk or water
350g (12oz) dessert apples (Cox's Orange Pippin)
1 teaspoon sugar
4 tablespoons cream
15–25g butter
Salt and freshly ground black pepper

Celeriac or root celery is great with pheasant, venison, duck or a juicy pork cutlet; you can also roast them, make them into gratins, soups, crisps...

Cut the peeled celeriac into large chunks. Simmer in the milk or lightly salted water until soft and tender, about 15 minutes. Meanwhile, peel and core the apples, cut into quarters and cook with the sugar and very little water (about 2 teaspoons) in a covered saucepan.

When the celeriac is cooked, drain and add to the apple. Purée in a food processor with the cream and a lump of butter until smooth. Taste and season with salt and pepper. This purée can of course be prepared ahead. Reheat in a covered dish in a moderate oven (180°C/350°F/gas mark 4).

Piquant Beetroot

SERVES 6

685g (1¹/₂lb) beetroot, cooked
15g (¹/₂oz) butter
Salt and freshly ground black pepper
A few drops of freshly squeezed lemon juice
Sugar
140–175ml (5–6fl oz) cream

Peel the cooked beetroot wearing rubber gloves if you are vain!

Chop the beetroot intro cubes.

Melt the butter in a sauté pan, add the beetroot and toss. Then add the freshly squeezed lemon juice and cream and allow to bubble for a few minutes. Season with salt, pepper and sugar. Taste, and add a little more lemon juice if necessary. Serve immediately.

Chinese Artichokes

SERVES 6

450g (1lb) Chinese artichokes
25–55g (1–2oz) butter
Salt and freshly ground black pepper
Chopped parsley, or a mixture of parsley and marjoram

Chinese artichoke looks beautiful but needs careful washing. The flavour, though, makes it worth the effort. Growing the plant is very rewarding as it increases every year.

Wash the artichokes, preferably as soon as they have been dug. Top and tail them. Melt a little butter in a saucepan, add the artichokes. Season with salt and freshly ground pepper, add a few tablespoons of water, cover with a butterwrapper and the lid of a saucepan. Cook on a medium heat for 5–15 minutes or until they are just tender. Add a little chopped parsley or a mixture of parsley and marjoram and serve.

Oven-roasted Winter Vegetables

About equal volume of parsnips, swede
turnips, celeriac and carrot, peeled and
cut into 1cm (1/2in) cubes
Olive oil
Salt and freshly ground black pepper

GARNISH
Freshly chopped winter herbs – thyme,
rosemary, chives and parsley

*In California, many restaurants have wood-burning ovens which give the
food a delicious sweet flavour. We now have one, too, in the garden café.*

Preheat the oven to 200°C/400°F/gas mark 6. Drizzle olive oil generously
over the cubed vegetables, season well with salt and pepper. Spread
them in a single layer in one or more roasting tins. Roast, uncovered, in the
preheated oven, stirring occasionally until they are fully cooked and just
beginning to caramelize. Take care, a little colour makes the vegetables
taste sweeter, but there's a fine line between caramelizing and burning:
too dark and they become bitter. Serve sprinkled with the winter herbs.

Christmas Semi-freddo with Raisins and Marrons Glacés

SERVES 10–12

80ml (3fl oz) Jamaica rum
100g (4oz) good-quality raisins
4 free-range eggs
55g (2oz) caster sugar
450g (1lb) sweetened chestnut purée
(crème de marrons)
1 teaspoon pure vanilla essence
200g (7oz) marrons glacés, roughly
chopped
425ml (14fl oz) cream

DECORATION
Whipped cream
6–8 marrons glacés

Chocolate Caraque (see page 189)

Sprig of holly
Icing sugar

YOU WILL NEED
A 2.3 litre (4 pint) pudding bowl

This is a wonderfully festive Italian semi-freddo.

Line the pudding bowl with a double thickness of cling film

Put the rum and raisins in a small saucepan, warm until the rum almost reaches boiling point and then turn off the heat and let the raisins plump up and cool in the rum.

Meanwhile, separate the eggs and beat the yolks with the caster sugar until light and fluffy. Stir the chestnut purée, vanilla essence, cold plump raisins, rum and roughly chopped marrons glacés into the egg yolks. Mix gently but thoroughly, then refrigerate while you whip the cream and egg whites.

Whip the cream and chill. Whisk the egg whites stiffly. Fold the whipped cream into the rum and raisin mixture, then fold in the stiffly beaten egg whites. Pour gently into the lined pudding bowl. Cover and freeze for at least 8 hours or overnight.

To serve: turn out on to a chilled serving dish. Remove the cling film and decorate with whipped cream, marrons glacés and Chocolate Caraque, top with a sprig of holly then dredge with icing sugar.

Chocolate Cases filled with Silky Chocolate Mousse

SERVES 10

CHOCOLATE CASES
225g (8oz) best-quality dark chocolate (find one with a high percentage of cocoa solids)
24 paper bun cases (use 2 papers for each chocolate case to give extra strength to the sides)

CHOCOLATE MOUSSE
225g (8oz) best quality dark chocolate (with a high percentage of cocoa solids)
15g (¹/₂oz) unsalted butter
150ml (¹/₄ pint) water
1 tablespoon Jamaica rum
6 small or 4 large free-range eggs

DECORATION
Whipped cream
Chocolate Caraque (see page 189)
Unsweetened cocoa powder

This is really rich, really sinful and really good!

First make the chocolate cases. Melt the chocolate until smooth in a very slow oven or in a bowl over hot water. Spread the chocolate evenly over the paper cases with the back of a teaspoon. Check that there are no 'see-through' patches when you hold them up to the light (it is a good idea to do a few extra cases to allow for accidents!). Stand each one in a bun tray and leave to firm in a cold place. Peel the paper layers off carefully and set aside.

Next make the mousse. Break the chocolate into small pieces and put in a bowl to melt with the butter and water over a low heat. Stir gently until melted and completely smooth. Remove from the heat and leave to cool, then whisk in the rum, if using, and the egg yolks. Whisk the egg whites and fold them in. Beat for 5–6 minutes: this makes the mousse smooth and silky. (Even though it sounds like a contradiction, the mousse thickens as it is beaten at the end.) Fill each chocolate case with the mousse. Allow to set for 5–6 hours or overnight.

Then make the Chocolate Caraque.

To serve: pipe a rosette of softly whipped cream on to each mousse. Top with a few pieces of Caraque. Sift a little unsweetened cocoa powder over the top and serve chilled.

171

Yoghurt and Cardamom with Pomegranate Seeds perfumed with Rose Blossom Water

SERVES 8-10

$1/4$ teaspoon green cardamom seeds, freshly ground – you'll need about 8–10 cardamom pods, depending on size
230ml (8fl oz) milk
175–200g (6–7oz) caster sugar
200ml (7fl oz) cream
3 rounded teaspoons powdered gelatine
425ml (15fl oz) natural yoghurt

POMEGRANATE SEEDS WITH ROSE BLOSSOM WATER
6–8 pomegranates depending on size
A little lemon juice
1–2 tablespoon caster sugar
Rose blossom water to taste

DECORATION
Sweet geranium or mint leaves

I've got a wonderful Irish rose called Souvenir de St Ann's in Lydia's garden. This rose blooms even in the depths of winter so I steal a few petals and crystallize them to decorate this and other desserts (see Crystallized Violets, page 48).

In summer you can serve this with sugared strawberries or mango, tossed with lime juice. It is also good with Gooseberry and Elderflower Compote (see page 42) or a compote of blood oranges or Kumquats (see page 173).

Remove the seeds from the cardamom pods and crush in a pestle and mortar. Put the milk, sugar and cream into a stainless steel saucepan with the ground cardamom. Stir until the sugar has dissolved and the mixture is warm to the touch. Remove from the heat and leave to infuse while you dissolve the gelatine.

Put 3 tablespoons of cold water into a small bowl, sprinkle the gelatine over the water, and allow to 'sponge' for a few minutes. Put the bowl into a saucepan of simmering water until the gelatine has melted and is completely clear. Add a little of the cardamom infused milk mixture, stir well and then mix this into the rest. Whisk the yoghurt lightly until smooth and creamy and stir into the cardamom mixture. Pour into a wide serving dish or a lightly oiled ring mould and leave to set for several hours.

Meanwhile, cut the pomegranates in half around the 'equator'. Carefully separate the seeds from the membrane. Put the seeds into a bowl, sprinkle with just a little freshly squeezed lemon juice and add caster sugar and rose blossom water to taste. Put in the refrigerator until well chilled.

If the yoghurt and cardamom have been set in a ring mould, turn out on to a chilled plate. Fill the centre with chilled, rose-scented pomegranate seeds. Decorate with sweet geranium or mint leaves or, even prettier, with crystallized rose petals.

Ballymaloe Vanilla Ice-cream with Kumquat Compote and Chocolate Diamonds

SERVES 6–8

VANILLA ICE-CREAM
2 free-range egg yolks
55g (2oz) sugar
125ml (4fl oz) water
$^1/_2$ teaspoon pure vanilla essence
600ml (1 pint) softly whipped cream
(measurement of cream when whipped)

KUMQUAT COMPOTE
1.5kg (3$^1/_2$lb) kumquats
1 litre (1$^3/_4$ pints) water
500g (1lb 2oz) sugar

CHOCOLATE DIAMONDS
225g (8oz) best quality dark chocolate
(with a high percentage of cocoa solids)

DECORATION
Fresh or crystallized mint leaves (optional)

For a fancy presentation to dazzle the pals at a dinner party: chill the serving plates. Allow the ice-cream to soften a little before shaping it into almond shapes, using two spoons or an ice-cream scoop. Arrange three on their sides in a flower shape on the chilled plates. Better still do this ahead and chill again before finishing. Spoon a little compote between the almond shapes of ice-cream and arrange a diamond-shaped piece of chocolate on its side in the gaps. Pop a sprig of fresh or crystallized mint in the centre and serve immediately – a delicious combination of flavours. For a less stressful presentation serve the ice-cream and compote simply in chilled bowls and offer the chocolate diamonds separately – equally delicious but not quite so dramatic.

The quality of cream which has real flavour and the quality of good, fresh free-range eggs is the secret of a good ice-cream and, in this instance, a pure vanilla essence.

First make the ice-cream. Put the egg yolks into a bowl and whisk until light and fluffy (keep the whites for meringues). Combine the sugar and water in a small heavy-bottomed saucepan and stir over heat until the sugar is completely dissolved; then remove the spoon and boil the syrup until it reaches the 'thread' stage, 106–113°C/223–236°F. It will look thick and syrupy; when a metal spoon is dipped in, the last drops of syrup will form thin threads. Pour this boiling syrup in a steady stream on to the egg yolks, whisking all the time. Add the vanilla essence and continue to whisk until it becomes a thick creamy white mousse. Fold the softly whipped cream into the mousse, pour into a bowl, cover and freeze for at least 6 hours.

Meanwhile, poach the fruit. Slice the kumquats into four circles and remove the pips. Put the kumquats into a saucepan with the water and sugar and cover the pan. Let them cook very gently for about half an hour. Cool and chill in the refrigerator until needed.

Next make the chocolate diamonds. Melt the chocolate in a very slow oven or in an oven proof glass bowl over barely simmering water. Spread the melted chocolate fairly thickly over a sheet of silicone paper. Leave to get cold and firm before cutting into strips about 2.5cm (1in) wide and then into diamonds at an angle.

Decorate with the mint leaves, if using.

Blood Orange Tart

SERVES 8

PASTRY
175g (6oz) white flour
1 tablespoon caster sugar
85g (3oz) butter
About 2 tablespoons orange juice or water
1 free-range egg yolk

FILLING
85g (3oz) butter
100g (3¹/₂oz) caster sugar
1 whole free-range egg and
2 free-range egg yolks
85g (3oz) ground almonds
1 tablespoon Grand Marnier

DECORATION
6 blood oranges

4–6 tablespoons Apricot Glaze
(see page 86)

YOU WILL NEED
25cm (10in) tart tin with removable base

Of all the citrus fruits, blood oranges excite me most. They appear in our shops for only about four weeks from the end of January, so we use them in juices and cocktails, fruit salads, tarts, sorbets, granitas, Buck's Fizz...

Preheat the oven to 180°C/350°F/gas mark 4.

Sieve the flour into a bowl and add the sugar. Cut the cold butter into cubes and rub into the dry ingredients until the mixture resembles coarse breadcrumbs. Mix the orange juice or water with the egg yolk and use to bind the pastry. Add a little more water if necessary but don't make it too sticky. Wrap and refrigerate for 30 minutes or so. Roll out the pastry and line the tart tin. Fill with baking beans and bake blind for 20–25 minutes.

Meanwhile, make the filling. Cream the butter, add the caster sugar and beat until light and fluffy. Add the eggs, beat well and then stir in the ground almonds and the liqueur.

When the tart shell is par-baked, allow to cool. Brush the base with apricot glaze and fill with the almond mixture, return to the oven and bake for about 20 minutes or until cooked and firm to the touch in the centre as well as at the sides.

Meanwhile, remove the peel and pith from the blood oranges and divide into segments. Drain and arrange in a pattern on top of the warm tart. Alternatively, slice the peeled oranges into thin rounds and arrange slightly overlapping on top of the warm tart. This looks prettiest but is slightly trickier to slice. Either way paint the oranges evenly with apricot glaze.

Serve warm with a bowl of softly whipped cream.

Marzipan Apple Tart

SERVES 8–10

**1 x 23cm (9in) Shortcrust Pastry tart shell
(see page 183)**

MARZIPAN
225g (8oz) caster sugar
65ml (2¹/₂fl oz) water
175g (6oz) ground almonds
1 drop of natural almond essence
1 free-range egg white

2–3 Bramley apples
15g (¹/₂oz) butter
1 teaspoon cinnamon, freshly ground
25g (1oz) caster sugar

YOU WILL NEED
1 x 23cm (9in) tart tin with removable base

This recipe keeps so well.

First make the shortcrust pastry; rest it for 30 minutes in a refrigerator if time allows.

Preheat the oven to 180°C/350°F/gas mark 4.

Roll out the pastry thinly and line the tart tin. Line with greaseproof paper and fill the shell with baking beans. Bake blind in the preheated oven for 15–20 minutes.

Meanwhile make the marzipan. Dissolve the sugar in the water and bring it to the boil. Cook to 116°C/240°F or to the 'soft ball' stage, keeping the sides of the saucepan brushed down with water. Remove from the heat and stir the syrup until cloudy. Add the ground almonds, essence and slightly beaten egg white. Mix very thoroughly. Pour into the tart base if ready; alternatively, pour into a bowl and spread over the tart base later.

Peel the apples, cut into quarters and core. Slice the apples into scant 5mm (¹/₄in) slices and arrange in overlapping circles over the marzipan in the tart. Brush lightly with the melted butter. Mix the cinnamon with the caster sugar. Sprinkle over the apples. Bake in the preheated oven for about 35 minutes.

Serve warm or cold with softly whipped cream.

Walnut Tart with Armagnac

SERVES 8–10

PASTRY
225g (8oz) flour
Pinch of salt
115g (4oz) butter
55g (2oz) caster sugar
2 free-range egg yolks
Few drops of vanilla essence (optional)

WALNUT FILLING
175g (6oz) freshly shelled walnuts
350ml (12fl oz) cream
1/2 teaspoon pure vanilla essence
115g (4oz) caster sugar
Pinch of salt
2 small free-range egg whites

ICING
3 tablespoons Armagnac or brandy
175g (6oz) icing sugar

DECORATION
16 walnut halves

YOU WILL NEED
1 x 25cm (10in) tart tin, preferably with removable base

Every autumn we buy a sack of walnuts from Mr Bell in the Cork market – it's a heck of a lot more labour-intensive to have to crack each nut but it's worth it to be sure of fresh rather than rancid walnuts. Delicious warm or cold, this winter tart keeps for up to a week.

Make the biscuit pastry in the usual way. I don't bother with a bowl, I just sieve the flour with a pinch of salt on to the clean work top and make a well in the centre with the back of my hand. Cut the butter into small cubes and add with the sugar, egg yolks and a few drops of vanilla essence, if using. With the fingertips of one hand, work these ingredients together until well mixed (the texture will resemble scrambled eggs), then quickly draw in the flour running your fingers through the mixture to coat the particles of butter and egg. Form the mixture into a line, with the heel of the hand knead the pastry away from you in quick rhythmic movements. Gather up the mixture again and repeat twice more, by which time the pastry should be perfectly amalgamated. Finally knead lightly to get into a smooth ball. Then roll it into a flat round, cover with cling film and leave to rest in the refrigerator for 1 hour. (If this all sounds too messy, you can make the pastry in a food processor or a bowl.)

Preheat the oven to 180°C/350°F/gas mark 4.

Roll out the pastry and line a 25cm (10in) tart tin. Line with greaseproof paper and fill with baking beans. Bake blind in the preheated oven for about 10 minutes, then remove the paper and cook for a further 5 minutes until golden and firm (this pastry must not brown or it will taste bitter).

Meanwhile, make the filling. Chop the walnuts roughly and add the cream, vanilla essence, caster sugar and a pinch of salt. When the tart shell is ready, fold the stiffly beaten egg whites into the filling and pour into the pre-baked tart shell. Return the tart to the oven at 180°C/350°F/gas mark 4, for about 45 minutes or until set and pale golden.

Meanwhile, make the icing: simply mix the Armagnac or brandy with the sifted icing sugar to make thickish icing.

When the tart is cooked, leave it to cool a little in the tin. Then transfer to a wire rack. While still slightly warm, pour the icing over and spread gently and evenly with a small palette knife. Decorate with walnut halves and serve with a bowl of softly whipped cream.

Agen Prunes stuffed with Walnuts and Rosewater Cream

SERVES 6

450g (1lb) Agen prunes, pitted
Same number of fresh walnut halves
About 150ml (¹/₄ pint) each red wine and
water or 300ml (¹/₂ pint) water
300ml (¹/₂ pint) cream
2 tablespoons caster sugar
1 tablespoon rose blossom water

DECORATION
A few chopped walnuts
Rose petals (optional)

This ancient Arab recipe from the Middle East will change your opinion of prunes – a pretty and delicious dish that tastes even better next day. We have experimented with taking out the stones from both soaked and dry prunes; unsoaked worked best. Claudia Roden originally introduced me to this recipe when she taught at the school.

Use a small knife to cut out the stones from the prunes and then stuff each with half a walnut. Arrange in a single layer in a sauté pan. Cover with a mixture of wine and water. Put the lid on the pan and simmer for about 30 minutes. Add more liquid if they become a little dry. They should be plump and soft. Lift them gently on to a serving plate in a single layer and let them cool.

Whip the cream to soft peaks and add the caster sugar and rose blossom water. Spoon blobs over the prunes and chill well. Just before serving, scatter a few chopped walnuts over each blob of cream, sprinkle with rose petals and serve well chilled.

Focaccia with Caramelized Onions, Cashel Blue Cheese and Walnuts

SERVES 1–2

FOR THE CARAMELIZED ONIONS
2–3 tablespoons olive oil
5 onions, thinly sliced

One-third recipe for Ballymaloe White Yeast Bread (see page 180) – about 400g (14oz) dough
Semolina or cornmeal

85–115g (3–4oz) Cashel Blue cheese
25–55g (1–2oz) walnuts, roughly chopped

We make many many types of bread at Ballymaloe Cookery School. This one can be served as a starter or a nibble or even, with bread and cheese, as a meal. Make the Ballymaloe White Yeast Bread (see page 180), use a third of the dough and make the remainder into crusty rolls. I have used Cashel Blue here but you can just as well use Stilton or Gorgonzola.

Preheat the oven to 230°C/450°F/gas mark 8

First make the caramelized onions. Heat the olive oil in a heavy saucepan, toss in the onions and cook on a low heat so that they soften and lightly caramelize to a pale golden brown (say 20–30 minutes).

Roll out the dough to 1cm (¹/₂in) thickness, 30cm (12in) in diameter. Sprinkle some semolina or cornmeal on to the pizza paddle and place the dough on top. Put on to an oiled baking sheet. Make indentations all over the surface with your finger tips. Cover the surface of the dough to within 2.5cm (³/₄in) of the edge with caramelized onions. Crumble the Cashel Blue cheese and scatter over the top, then sprinkle with chopped walnuts. Drizzle with a little olive oil and bake in the preheated oven. Bake for 20 minutes and serve immediately.

Wheaten Bread

Wheaten breads or soda breads are very fast to make and are still made widely throughout the Irish countryside. Buttermilk is for sale in every village shop. Flavour varies according to the type of flour, recipe and of course the 'turn of hand' of the baker. The traditional loaf is shaped into a round and then scored into quarters. A cross is then made with the tip of a knife – to let the fairies out, so they won't jinx your bread. The fairies are very active in Ireland particularly around Hallowe'en; none of us to this day would dream of making a loaf of Irish wheaten or soda bread without letting the fairies out, it's part of what we are!

MAKES 1 LARGE ROUND LOAF

575g (1¼lb) brown wholemeal flour
(preferably stone-ground)
575g (1¼lb) plain white flour
2 teaspoons salt
2 teaspoons bread soda
(bicarbonate of soda), sieved
Up to 850ml (1½ pints) sour milk
or buttermilk

Preheat the oven to 230°C/450°F/gas mark 8.

Mix the dry ingredients well together. Make a well in the centre and add about 750ml (25fl oz) of the sourmilk or buttermilk. Working from the centre, mix with your hand and add more milk if necessary. The dough should be soft but not sticky. Turn out on to a floured board, wash and dry your hands. Sprinkle them with flour and then tidy the dough just enough to shape into a round. Flatten slightly to about 5cm (2in). Put on to a floured baking sheet. Mark with a deep cross and bake in a the preheated oven for 15–20 minutes, then reduce the temperature to 200°C/400°F/gas mark 6 for about 20–25 minutes or until the bread is cooked and sounds hollow when tapped. Cool on a wire rack.

Note: you could add 25g (1oz) fine oatmeal, 1 egg and 25g (1oz) butter to the above to make a richer wheaten dough.

Lovisa's Swedish Crispbread

MAKES ABOUT 20

2 teaspoons caraway seeds
50g (1¾ oz) fresh yeast
500ml (17fl oz) tepid milk
600g (1lb 5oz) plain rye flour (sometimes more)
600g (1lb 5oz) white flour
225g (8oz) coarse rye flour (for dusting the board)
2 teaspoons salt

YOU WILL NEED

2.5cm (1in) cutter

I came home from my maiden trip to Norway in 1995 armed with a spiky rolling pin and the taste memories of many delicious Norwegian foods, including their thin flat crispbread. As luck would have it, I had a lovely Swedish girl on my new Certificate course. One day she told me that her mother had just sent her a recipe for the crispbread that she missed so much. Did I have any rye flour and could she make it at the school? I couldn't believe my luck – she couldn't believe her eyes when she discovered a Knackebrod rolling pin in Shanagarry! The crispbread is so delicious that we asked for the recipe on the first bite. It would keep for weeks if you could resist nibbling it constantly.

Preheat the oven to 180°C/350°F/gas mark 4.

Grind the caraway seeds finely in a pestle and mortar.

Crumble the yeast and pour the tepid milk over it. Mix the flours with the salt and the caraway seeds. Sieve the flours into the liquid and stir with a wooden spoon. Gather the dough together and turn on to a floured board. Shape the dough into a thick rope and divide into twenty pieces. Knead the pieces into balls, cover and leave to rise for 20 minutes.

Sprinkle the coarse rye flour on to the board. Roll out each ball with a smooth rolling pin and then roll with the spiky rolling pin. (Alternatively, prick each flat bread with a fork.)

Turn the dough to keep in a round and roll out to a circle, about 20cm (8in). Lovisa stamps out a little hole in the centre of each crispbread in the traditional way with a 2.5cm (1in) cutter.

Bake on a lightly greased tray in the preheated oven for 8–10 minutes. Cool on a wire rack. Eat warm or cold.

Ballymaloe White Yeast Bread

MAKES 2 X 450G (1LB) LOAVES

20g (³/₄oz) fresh yeast
About 450ml (³/₄ pint) water
25g (1oz) butter
2 teaspoons salt
15g (¹/₂oz) sugar
675g (1¹/₂lb) strong white flour
Egg wash or 1 free-range egg yolk and
2 tablespoons of cream beaten together
Poppy or sesame seeds (optional)

YOU WILL NEED
2 x 450g (1lb) loaf tins, brushed with
non-scented oil

We make this dough into plaits and use the base for pizzas (substitute olive oil for the butter), rolls and loaves.

Mix the yeast with 150ml (1/4 pint) of lukewarm water until it dissolves. Put the butter, salt and sugar into a bowl with 150ml (1/4 pint) of very hot water, stir until the sugar and salt are dissolved and the butter has melted. Add 150ml (1/4 pint) of cold water. By now, the liquid should be lukewarm or at blood heat, so combine with the yeast.

Sieve the flour into a bowl, make a well in the centre and pour in most of the lukewarm liquid. Mix to a loose dough adding the remaining liquid, or more flour or water if necessary. Turn the dough on to a floured board, cover and leave to relax for 5–10 minutes. Then knead vigorously for about 10 minutes or until smooth and springy (if kneading in a food mixer with a dough hook, 5 minutes is usually long enough).

Put the dough to rise in a pottery or delph bowl and cover tightly with cling film. Yeast dough rises best in a warm, moist atmosphere: near your cooker or on top of a radiator is a good spot. However, if your kitchen is warm enough for you, the bread will rise in its own time, about 2–3 hours.

When the dough has more than doubled in size, knead again for about 2–3 minutes until all the air has been forced out – this is called 'knocking back'. Leave the dough to relax again for 10 minutes.

Preheat the oven to 230°C/450°F/gas mark 8.

Shape the bread into loaves, plaits or rolls, sprinkle with poppy or sesame seeds if you desire and cover with a light tea towel. Leave to rise again in a warm place; this rising will be much shorter (only about 20–30 minutes). It is ready for baking when a small dent remains if pressed lightly with a finger. Brush with egg wash or egg and cream glaze or simply with water.

Bake in the preheated oven for 30–35 minutes. Remove from the tins about 10 minutes before the end of baking and return to the oven to bake the crust underneath. Cool on a wire rack.

White Soda Bread

MAKES 1 BIG LOAF

450g (1lb) white flour, unbleached
1 teaspoon salt
1 teaspoon bread soda
Sour milk or buttermilk to mix – about
350–375ml (12–13fl oz)

Soda bread only takes 2–3 minutes to make and 20–30 minutes to bake. It is certainly another of my 'great convertibles', and we have had the greatest fun experimenting with different variations and uses. This kind of bread is also great with olives, sun dried tomatoes or caramelized onions added, so the possibilities are endless for the hitherto humble soda bread.

Preheat the oven to 230°C/450°F/gas mark 8

Sieve the dry ingredients into a bowl and make a well in the centre. Pour most of the milk in at once. Using one hand, mix in the flour from the sides of the bowl, adding more milk if necessary. The dough should be softish, not too wet and sticky. When it all comes together, turn it out on to a floured board, knead lightly for a second, just enough to tidy it up. Pat the dough into a round about 2.5cm (1in) deep and cut a cross on it to let the fairies out! Let the cuts go over the sides of the bread to make sure of this. Bake in a hot oven, 230°C/450°F/ gas mark 8 for 20 minutes, then turn the temperature down to 200°C/400°F/gas mark 6 for 15 minutes or until cooked. If you are in doubt, tap the bottom of the bread: if it is cooked, it will sound hollow.

White Soda Scones

Make the dough as above, flattening the dough into a round about 2.5cm (1in) deep. Cut into scones. Cook for about 20 minutes in a hot oven (see above).

White Soda Bread with Herbs

Add 2 tablespoons of freshly chopped herbs, such as rosemary or sage, thyme, chives, parsley and lemon balm to the dry ingredients and continue as above. Shape into a loaf or scones and bake as for White Soda Bread.

Basic Recipes

In this section we've gathered together all the miscellaneous recipes referred to in the main chapters of the book.

Ballymaloe French Dressing

Never swamp salads with dressing: use just enough to make the leaves glisten. Green salads must not be dressed until just before serving, otherwise they become tired and unappetizing.

55ml (2fl oz) wine vinegar
150ml (6fl oz) olive oil (or a mixture of olive and either sunflower or groundnut oils)
1 level teaspoon mustard (Dijon or English)
1 large clove of garlic
1 small spring onion
sprig of parley, sprig of watercress
1 level teaspoon of salt
Few grinds of black pepper

Put all the ingredients into a blender and run at medium speed for about a minute. Alternatively, mix the oil and vinegar in a bowl to emulsify, add the mustard, salt, freshly ground pepper and mashed garlic. Finely chop the parsley, spring onion and watercress and add in. Whisk before using.

Grainy Mustard Sauce

Quick to make and delicious with pork.

230ml (8fl oz) cream
1 dessertspoon smooth mustard
1 tablespoon grainy mustard
Salt and freshly ground black pepper

Put the cream and both mustards in a small pan and bring slowly to the boil, stirring occasionally. Taste and season if necessary.

Roux

Roux can be stored in a cool place (up to two weeks in a refrigerator), or made up as and when required. Whisk into boiling liquid to thicken sauces, gravies, stews, etc.

115g (4oz) butter
115g (4oz) flour

Melt the butter and stir in the flour. Cook for 2 minutes on a low heat, stirring occasionally.

Béchamel Sauce

This is wonderfully quick to make, if you already have Roux prepared.

300ml ($\frac{1}{2}$ pint) milk
A few slices of carrot
A few slices of onion
3 peppercorns
Small sprig of thyme
Small sprig of parsley
40g (1$\frac{1}{2}$ oz) Roux (see previous recipe)
Salt and freshly ground black pepper

Put the milk into a pan with the carrot, onion, peppercorns, and herbs. Bring to the boil, and simmer for 4–5 minutes. Remove from the heat and leave to nfuse for 10 minutes. Strain out the vegetables, bring the milk back to the boil. Whisk in the Roux to thicken to a light coating consistency. Season to taste.

Hollandaise Sauce

Delectable with asparagus or fish.

2 egg yolks, preferably free-range
125g (4oz) butter, cut into dice
1 dessertspoon cold water
About 1 teaspoon lemon juice

Put the egg yolks into a heavy-bottomed stainless-steel pan on a very low heat, add the cold water and thoroughly whisk. Gradually add the cubed butter – as one piece melts, add the next – whisking all the time. The mixture will gradually thicken; if it begins to scramble or become too thick, remove from the heat; add a little more cold water if necessary.

Don't leave the pan or stop whisking until the sauce is complete. Finally, add the lemon juice to taste. Pour into a bowl and keep warm over a pan of hot but not boiling water.

Tomato Fondue

Tomato Fondue is one of our great convertibles. It has a number of uses – as a vegetable, sauce, filling for omelette, topping for pizza, stuffing and so on. Cook it quickly for a fresh taste or slowly for a stronger taste, particularly if you are using tinned tomatoes. It is great with green chillies added. We often toss French beans in it.

1 tablespoon olive oil
115g (4oz) onions, sliced
1 clove garlic, crushed
900g (2lb) very ripe tomatoes (peeled) in summer, or use tinned ones in winter
Salt and freshly ground black pepper
Sugar
About 1 tablespoon freshly chopped mint or torn basil

Heat the oil in a non-reactive saucepan. Add the sliced onions and garlic, toss until coated and cook, covered, on a low heat until soft. It is vital that the onions are completely soft before the tomatoes are added. Slice the fresh or tinned tomatoes and add to the pan with all the juices. Season with salt, pepper and sugar (tinned tomatoes need lots of sugar because of their high acidity). Add a generous sprinkling of chopped mint or torn basil. Cook, uncovered, for 10–20 minutes or more, or until the tomato softens.

Vine-ripened Tomato Purée

Tomato Purée is one of the very best ways of preserving the flavour of ripe summer tomatoes for winter to use in soups, stews and casseroles. We make heaps of it at the end of August when we have a glut of tomatoes which burst with flavour. Make lots and freeze it to help you through the winter.

900g (2lb) vine-ripened tomatoes
1 small onion, chopped
Good pinch of salt
A few twists of black pepper
2 teaspoons sugar

Cut the very ripe tomatoes into quarters and put into a stainless steel saucepan with the onion, salt, pepper and sugar. Cook on a gentle heat until the tomatoes are soft (no water is needed). Put through the fine blade of a mouli-légume or a nylon sieve. Leave to get cold, refrigerate or freeze.

Puff Pastry

Home-made puff pastry takes a little time to make but it is more than worth the effort for its wonderful flavour that bears no relation to the commercial equivalent. It is essential to use butter.

MAKES ABOUT 1.2KG (2LB 12OZ)

450g (1lb) chilled plain flour (use strong or baker's flour if possible)
Pinch of salt
Squeeze of lemon juice (optional)
300–350ml (10–12fl oz) cold water
450g (1lb) butter, firm but pliable

Sieve the chilled flour and salt into a bowl and mix to a firm dough with water and a squeeze of lemon juice if liked. This dough is called détrempe. Cover with greaseproof paper or cling film and rest for 30 minutes in the refrigerator.

Roll the détrempe into a square about 1cm (^{1}/2in) thick. If the butter is very hard, beat it (still in the wrapper) with a rolling pin until pliable but not sticky.

Unwrap the butter and shape into a slab roughly 2cm (^{3}/4in) thick; place in the centre of the dough and then fold the dough over the edges of the butter to make a neat parcel. Make sure your chilled marble slab or pastry board is well-floured, then flatten the dough with a rolling pin and continue to roll until you have a rectangle about 45cm (18in) long and 15cm (6in) wide (these measurements don't need to be exact).

Fold into three to make an oblong with the edges aligned as accurately as you can. Seal the edges with a rolling pin.

Give the dough a quarter turn: it should now be on your board as if it were a book with its length pointing away from you. Roll again, fold in three and seal the edges with the rolling pin as before. Cover with greaseproof paper or cling film and rest the pastry in the refrigerator for at least 30 minutes before use.

Shortcrust Pastry

You need to keep eveything as cool as possible: if the fat is allowed to melt the finished pastry may be tough.

MAKES ENOUGH FOR A 23CM (9IN)
DIAMETER PASTRY SHELL

200g (7oz) flour
2 teaspoons caster sugar
110g (4oz) cold butter, cut into small cubes
1 egg yolk, preferably free-range
3–4 tablespoons cold water

Sieve the flour and sugar into a bowl, and rub in the cubed butter with your fingertips. When the mixture looks like coarse breadcrumbs, stop. Whisk the egg yolk and add the water.

Using a fork or knife to combine, add just enough liquid to bring the pastry together, then discard the fork and collect the pastry into a ball with your hands. This way you can judge more accurately if you need a few more drops of egg liquid. Although slightly damp pastry is easier to handle and roll out, the resulting crust can be tough and may well shrink out of shape as the water evaporates in the oven. Drier (and more difficult-to-handle) pastry will give a crisper shorter crust.

Cover the pastry with cling film and leave to rest in the fridge for a minimum of 15 minutes or, better still, 30 minutes. This will make the pastry much less elastic and easier to roll.

Polenta

Polenta is a most adaptable dish. It can be served hot, the moment it is cooked, or it can be turned into a wet dish, rinsed in cold water and allowed to get cold. It can then be sliced and char-grilled, pan-grilled, toasted or fried and served with all sorts of toppings. It can even be cut into thin slices and layered with a sauce just like lasagne.

SERVES 6–8

1.7 litres (3 pints) water
2 teaspoons salt
225g (8oz) coarse polenta flour (maize)
115g (4oz) butter
85–115g (3–4oz) freshly grated
Parmesan (Parmigiano Reggiano is best) (optional)
Sea salt and freshly ground black pepper

Put the water into a deep, heavy-bottomed saucepan and bring to the boil. Add the salt, then sprinkle in the polenta flour very slowly, letting it slip gradually through your fingers, whisking all the time (this should take about 3–4 minutes). Bring to the boil and when it starts to 'erupt like a volcano', turn the heat down to the absolute minimum – it's best to use a heat diffuser mat if you have one. Cook for about 40 minutes, stirring regularly. I use a whisk at the beginning but as soon as the polenta comes to the boil I change to a flat-bottomed wooden spoon. If you stir constantly on a slightly higher heat, the cooking time can be reduced to about 20 minutes, but the result is more digestible if cooked more slowly over a longer period. The polenta is cooked when it is very thick but not solid and comes away from the sides of the pot as you stir.

As soon as the polenta is cooked, stir in the butter, freshly grated Parmesan and lots of pepper. Taste and add a little more sea salt if necessary. The polenta should be soft and flowing: it it is a little too stiff, add some boiling water. Serve immediately. Try it with Sweet-sour Pork with Prunes, Raisins and Pine Kernels (see page 160).

Flavoured Oils and Vinegars

Herbs are at their most aromatic just before they flower. So in June and July we make our stock of infused oils and vinegars for the year. We started years ago with basil oil, when basil was rare and scarce – it was a way of preserving every last precious leaf. This led us to try other herbs, such as rosemary, sage, annual marjoram, oregano, and thyme leaves. Some herbs, including tarragon and dill, preserve better in vinegar; we have also had success with elderflower vinegar. Fruit vinegars work well too, but we make very little because in practice we used only small quantities after the initial novelty had worn off.

Herb oils and vinegars we use in much greater quantities and we discover more uses all the time. Chilli oil, roast garlic oil and dried mushroom oil have also become standard drizzles for everything from flavouring croutons to pasta, salads, soups, mashed potatoes, or just an addictive dipping oil for crusty bread.

In general, we are not very scientific in the way we make our flavoured oil. We simply pour out a little oil from the bottle, in most cases I use extra virgin olive oil – Lesieur or Puget are the brands we use large quantities of at present – and stuff the herbs down into the oil. The quantity varies depending on whether one wants a mild or strong flavour – experiment.

I am sure it would be more correct to wash and dry the herbs carefully but I have to say that I rarely do because the herbs come straight from the garden or greenhouse. We top up the bottles with oil and replace the lid tightly. I store basil oil in a refrigerator or cold room but the other oils sit on a shelf in the larder and kitchens. They are best left to infuse for a few days and then used within a matter of weeks, though again I have to say that many of our bottles have been around for months and were still fine but stronger and in some cases a little better in flavour.

Basil Oil

The basil can be used to flavour the oil or the oil may be used to preserve the basil depending on the quantity used.

Olive oil
Fresh basil leaves

Ensure the basil leaves are clean and dry. Pour a little of the olive oil out of the bottle, stuff at least 8–10 basil leaves into the bottle and top up with oil. Seal and store in a cold place.

Chilli Oil – Olio Picante

Stuff 1–6 dried chillies down into a bottle of oil, top up and leave to infuse for a few days before using.

Chilli, Herb and Pepper Oil

One of my favourite combinations is 1–2 chillies, a sprig or two of rosemary or annual marjoram and a teaspoon of black peppercorns. This is particularly good for brushing on steaks, lamb chops or chicken breasts for a barbecue.

Roasted Garlic Oil

The oil used to roast garlic (see page 83) is great stuff for cooking croutons or crostini, for drizzling over salads, into soups, vegetable stews, pasta and so on. Make in small quantities and use within a week because it can ferment.

Crostini

Crostini are very good made into Tapenade Toasts(see page 186).

Extra virgin olive oil for frying
Slices of French bread or ciabatta, 5mm (¼ in) thick, cut at an angle

Put 2.5cm (1in) olive oil in a pan and heat until very hot. Sauté the slices of French bread one at a time, turning as soon as they are golden and drain on kitchen paper.

Home-made Chicken Stock

Instead of flinging things into the bin, keep your poultry carcasses, giblets and vegetable trimmings and use them for your stock pot. Nowadays some supermarkets and poulterers are happy to give you chicken carcasses or giblets because there is so little demand.

This recipe is just a guideline. If you have just one carcass and don't want to make a small quantity of stock, freeze it until you have three or four carcasses and some giblets, then you can make a really good-sized pot of stock later.

Don't use chicken livers, which make stock bitter. There are also vegetables which should not be put in the stock pot: potatoes soak up the flavour and make the stock cloudy; parsnips are too strong, as are beetroot; cabbage and other brassicas can give an 'off-taste' after they have been cooked for a while. A little white turnip is sometimes an asset, but it is easy to overdo it. I also ban bayleaf in my chicken stocks as I find that the flavour of bay can easily predominate and add a sameness to all soups made from that stock.

MAKES ABOUT 3.4 LITRES (6 PINTS)

2–3 raw or cooked carcasses, or both
Chicken giblets – neck, heart, gizzard
About 3.4 litres (6 pints) water
1 onion, sliced
1 leek, split in two
1 outside stick of celery or 1 lovage leaf
1 carrot, sliced
A few parsley stalks
Sprig of thyme
6 peppercorns

Chop up the carcasses as much as possible. Put all the ingredients into a large saucepan and add enough cold water to cover. Bring to the boil and skim the fat off the top with a metal spoon. Simmer for 3–5 hours. Strain and remove any remaining fat. If you need a stronger flavour, boil down the liquid in an open pan to reduce by one-third or one-half of the volume. Do not add salt.

Note: stock will keep for several days in the refrigerator. If you want to keep it for longer, boil it up again for 5–6 minutes every couple of days; allow it to get cold and refrigerate again. Stock also freezes perfectly. For cheap containers you can use large yoghurt cartons or plastic milk bottles, which, if you are in a hurry, you can cut off the frozen stock. In restaurants, stock is usually allowed to simmer uncovered, so that it will be as clear as possible, but I usually advise people making stock at home to cover the pot, otherwise the whole house will smell of stock, which may put you off making it on a regular basis.

Salt is another ingredient that has no place in my home-made stocks. This is because a salted stock can easily become oversalted when it is reduced to make a sauce.

Home-made Duck Stock

This makes a simple stock and can be used as the basis of duck gravy.

Neck, gizzard, heart and any other trimmings
1 medium carrot, sliced
1 onion, quartered
Bouquet garni of parsley stalks, celery stick and thyme sprig
2 or 3 peppercorns

Follow the instructions for the Chicken Stock recipe (see page 184). Cover all the ingredients in a saucepan with cold water, bring slowly to the boil and simmer for 2–3 hours.

Basic Chinese Stock

This delicious stock forms the essential bases of many delicious light fish or meat soups. Equal quantities of chicken pieces and spare ribs can be used or 1.8kg (4lb) of either. The stock will keep in the refrigerator for several days; after that boil it every two or three days. It also freezes perfectly.

MAKES ABOUT 2 LITRES (3^1/$_2$ PINTS)

900g (2lb) chicken giblets, wings, necks, hearts, gizzards, etc.
900g (2lb) pork spare ribs
7cm (3in) piece fresh root ginger, unpeeled and thinly sliced
6 large spring onions
4.5–5.7 litres (7^1/$_2$–9^1/$_2$ pints) Home-made Chicken Stock (see page 184)
4 tablespoons Shao Hsing rice wine

Put all the ingredients, except the rice wine, in a large saucepan. Bring to the boil and skim off any scum. Cover and simmer for about 4 hours, skimming regularly. Add the rice wine 5 minutes before the end of the cooking time.

Strain the stock and leave to cool, then refrigerate. Remove the solidified fat from the top of the stock before use.

Home-made Vegetable Stock

This recipe is just a guide – you can make stock from almost any vegetable in season (although read the comments I make under the recipe for Chicken Stock on page 184), but try not to use too much of any one unless you want the flavour of that particular vegetable to predominate. This stock keeps for up to a week in a refrigerator.

MAKES ABOUT 2.2 LITRES (4 PINTS)

1 small white turnip
2 onions, peeled, or the green parts of 2–3 leeks
3 sticks of celery, scrubbed
3 large carrots, scrubbed
^{1}/$_2$ fennel bulb, roughly chopped
4–6 parsley stalks
2.5 litres (4^1/$_2$ pints) cold water
Bouquet garni
115g (4oz) mushrooms
A few peppercorns

Roughly chop all the vegetables and put all the ingredients into a large saucepan. Bring to the boil; then turn the heat down, cover the pan and leave to simmer for 1^1/$_2$–2 hours. Strain through a sieve.

Home-made Beef Stock

Brown beef stock is used for game stews and brown sauces as well as for beef dishes. This stock will keep for 2–3 days in the refrigerator. If you want to keep it for longer, boil it again for 10 minutes, and then chill once more. It can also be frozen.

MAKES ABOUT 4 LITRES (6^3/$_4$ PINTS)

2.25–2.7kg (5–6lb) beef bones, preferably with some scraps of meat on, cut into small pieces
2 large onions, quartered
2 large carrots, quartered
3 sticks celery, cut into 1cm (^{1}/$_2$ in) pieces
Large bouquet garni (parsley stalks, bay leaf, thyme and tarragon)
10 peppercorns
2 cloves
4 cloves garlic, unpeeled
1 teaspoon tomato purée
4 litres (6^3/$_4$ pints) water

Preheat the oven to 230°C/450°F/gas mark 8.

Put the bones into a roasting tin and roast for 30 minutes or until the bones are well browned. Add the onions, carrots and celery and return to the oven until the vegetables are also browned. Transfer the bones and vegetables to the stock pot with a metal spoon. Add the bouquet garni, the peppercorns, cloves, garlic and tomato purée. De-glaze the roasting tin with some water, bring to the boil and pour over the bones and the vegetables. Add the remaining water and bring to the boil slowly. Skim the stock and simmer gently for 5–6 hours.

Strain the stock, leave it to get cold, then refrigerate. Remove all the solidified fat from the top of the stock before use.

Pesto

Pesto is one of the new basics. It is extremely easy to make if you can get hold of any herbs. Even better grow your own as basil is so expensive. We grow so much basil. It really starts to grow in summer, you must pick it before the flowers blossom. The term pesto is becoming more and more elastic. Use culinary licence and experiment with new combinations; we love tomato and mint! Try using different herbs, olives and sun-dried tomatoes.

Pesto keeps for weeks in the refrigerator in a sterilized jar, covered with a generous layer of olive oil. Always use a clean spoon! It also freezes well but for best results don't add the grated Parmesan until it has defrosted. Eat it with pastas, drizzle it over fish or char-grilled chicken. And it really jazzes up a tomato salad in the winter.

MAKES ABOUT 400ML (14FL OZ)

115g (4oz) fresh basil leaves
150g (5fl oz) extra virgin olive oil
25g (1oz) fresh pine kernels (taste one to make sure they are not rancid)
2 large cloves garlic, peeled and crushed
55g (2oz) freshly and finely grated Parmesan cheese (preferably Parmigiano Reggiano)
Salt

In a food processor, whizz the basil with the olive oil, pine kernels and garlic, or pound them in a pestle and mortar. Remove to a bowl and fold in the Parmesan cheese. Taste and season with salt.

Variations
Mint and Parsley Pesto

Substitute 55g (2oz) fresh mint and 55g (2oz) fresh parsley for the basil in the above recipe.

Parsley Pesto

If you have not got any basil, parsley pesto is a good alternative. We make it throughout the winter, often spicing it with some chilli. It is marvellous drizzled over roast vegetables, fish or pan-grilled chicken. You may want to alter the proportion of olive oil.

MAKES ABOUT 240ML (8FL OZ)

25g (1oz) flat-leaf parsley (no stalks)
1–2 cloves garlic, peeled and crushed
40g (1$^{1}/_{2}$oz) freshly grated Parmesan cheese (Parmigiano Reggiano is best)
25g (1oz) pine kernels
75–150ml (3–5fl oz) extra virgin olive oil
Salt

Put all the ingredients, except the oil and salt, into a food processor. Whizz for a second or two, add the oil and a little salt. Taste to check the seasoning.

Tapenade

You can buy the olives whole for this recipe, and remove the stones yourself. You will need about 130g (5oz) of unpitted olives. Serve on Crostini (see page 182) as Tapenade Toasts.

SERVES 6–8

55g (2oz) anchovy fillets
100g (3$^{1}/_{2}$oz) stoned black Kalamata olives
1 tablespoon capers
1 teaspoon Dijon mustard
1 teaspoon freshly squeezed lemon juice
Freshly ground pepper
2–3 tablespoons extra virgin olive oil

Whizz up the anchovy fillets with the stoned black olives, capers, mustard, lemon juice and freshly ground pepper for just a few seconds in a food processor. Alternatively, use a pestle and mortar. When it becomes a coarse purée, slowly add the olive oil.

Horseradish Sauce

Horseradish grows wild in many parts of Britain and Ireland and looks like giant dock leaves. The roots, which you grate, can be dug up at any time of the year. If you cannot find any near you, plant some in your own garden but be careful because it spreads like mad and can become a pest. This is a fairly mild horseradish sauce. If you want to really clear the sinuses, increase the amounts of horseradish.

SERVES 8–10

1$^{1}/_{2}$ –3 tablespoons horseradish root, scrubbed, peeled and grated
2 teaspoons wine vinegar
1 teaspoon lemon juice
$^{1}/_{4}$ teaspoon mustard
$^{1}/_{4}$ teaspoon salt
Pinch of freshly ground black pepper
1 teaspoon sugar
240ml (8fl oz) softly whipped cream

Put the grated horseradish into a bowl with the vinegar, lemon juice, mustard, salt, pepper and sugar. Fold in the softly whipped cream but do not over-mix or the sauce will curdle. It keeps for 2–3 days but cover it tightly so that it does not pick up other flavours in the refrigerator.

Horseradish Mayonnaise

SERVES 6–8

2 free-range egg yolks
2 tablespoons Dijon mustard
1 tablespoon sugar
2 tablespoons wine vinegar
150ml ($^{1}/_{4}$ pint) light olive oil or sunflower oil
1 tablespoon grated fresh horseradish
1 rounded teaspoon freshly chopped parsley
1 rounded teaspoon freshly chopped tarragon

Put the eggs into a bowl, add the mustard, sugar and wine vinegar and mix well. Whisk in the oil gradually as you do when making mayonnaise. Finally, add the horseradish, parsley and tarragon. Taste and season if necessary. Serve with Carpaccio (see page 23) or smoked trout.

Sweet Dill Mayonnaise

1 large egg yolk, preferably free range
2 tablespoons French mustard
1 tablespoon white sugar
150ml (1/4 pint) groundnut or sunflower oil
1 tablespoon white wine vinegar
1 tablespoon finely chopped fresh dill
Salt and freshly ground black pepper

Whisk the egg yolk with the mustard and sugar, drip in the oil drop by drop, whisking all the time, then add the vinegar and fresh dill.

Cucumber Pickle

SERVES 8–12

500g (generous 1lb) thinly sliced unpeeled cucumber
1 medium onion, thinly sliced
175g (6oz) sugar
1 level tablespoon salt
230ml (8fl oz) cider vinegar
1 teaspoon mustard seed

Combine the cucumber and onion in a large bowl. Mix the sugar, salt, vinegar and mustard seed together and pour over the cucumber and onion slices. Place in a tighly covered container in the refrigerator and leave for at least 4–5 hours or overnight before using.

This relish keeps well for up to a week in the refrigerator.

Redcurrant Sauce

Serve this with guinea-fowl, chicken, turkey, bacon, ham and coarse pâtés.

SERVES 4–6

150g (5 1/4oz) sugar
125ml (4fl oz) water
140g (5oz) redcurrants

Put the sugar and water into a pan and stir until the sugar dissolves, then bring to the boil. Toss in the redcurrants, bring back to the boil and cook, uncovered, for 4–5 minutes or until the redcurrants burst. Serve hot or cold.

Bramley Apple Sauce

450g (1lb) Bramley Seedling cooking apples
1–2 dessertspoons water
55g (2oz) sugar, depending on the tartness of the apples

Peel, quarter and core the apples, cut the pieces into two and put in a stainless-steel or cast-iron pan with the sugar and water. Cover and put over a low heat. As soon as the apple has broken down, stir and taste for sweetness, adding a little more sugar if necessary.

Tomato and Coriander Salsa (Salsa Cruda)

This fresh sauce is ever present on Mexican tables.

SERVES 4–6

2 very ripe tomatoes, chopped
1 tablespoon chopped onion
1 clove garlic, crushed
1/2 –1 chilli, finely chopped

1–2 tablespoons freshly chopped coriander
Freshly squeezed lime juice
Salt and freshly ground black pepper
Sugar

Mix all the ingredients together. Season with salt, pepper and sugar.

Salsa Verde

SERVES 6–8

2 bunches Italian flat-leaf parsley
Zest and juice of 1–2 lemons
3 cloves garlic, crushed
2 teaspoons freshly grated horseradish
1 1/2 tablespoons salted capers, rinsed
Extra virgin olive oil
Salt and freshly ground black pepper

Put the parsley leaves, lemon zest, garlic, horseradish and capers in a food processor. Process in an on/off method until the mixture is finely chopped. (Alternatively, chop on a wooden board with a knife or mezzaluna.) Add the freshly squeezed lemon juice and enough olive oil to make a moist salsa. Season to taste with salt and pepper.

Guacamole

This in true Mexican style has no tomato in it. In Mexico the texture of guacamole differs from place to place – experiment until you find one you're happy with.

SERVES 2–4

1 ripe avocado, preferably Mexican
1 clove garlic, crushed
1–2 tablespoons freshly squeezed lime or (as a last resort) lemon juice
About 1 tablespoon olive oil (optional)
1 tablespoon chopped fresh coriander
Sea salt and freshly ground black pepper

Mash the flesh from the avocado with a fork or, in a pestle and mortar, with the garlic. Add the freshly squeezed lime juice, a little olive oil, coriander, salt and pepper to taste.

Mint Sauce

Traditional mint sauce made with tender young shoots of fresh mint takes only minutes to make. It is the perfect accompaniment to spring lamb. We are on tenterhooks at Easter, waiting for the first sprigs of mint to eat with the lamb. For those who are expecting a bright green jelly, the slightly dull colour and watery texture comes as a surprise. This is how it ought to be. Try it.

MAKES 180ML (6FL OZ)

2 tablespoons finely chopped fresh mint
2 tablespoons sugar
6–8 tablespoons boiling water
2 tablespoons white wine vinegar or
freshly squeezed lemon juice

Put the sugar and freshly chopped mint into a sauce-boat. Add the boiling water and vinegar or lemon juice. Leave to infuse for 5–10 minutes before serving.

Serve with Easter Lamb with Roast Spring Onions (see page 35).

Crispy Onions

These taste best when freshly cooked, but they may also be cooked in advance.

1 large onion
Milk
Well-seasoned flour
Sunflower oil for frying

Peel and slice the onion into 5mm (1/4in) rings. Separate the rings and cover with milk until needed. Heat the oil in a frying pan to 180°C/350°F. Toss the onion rings a few at a time in seasoned flour. Deep fry until golden in the hot oil. Spread them out on kitchen paper in a single layer and allow to get cold. (They are delicious: you'll need to hide them or they may disappear!) Just before serving, pop them into a hot oven, uncovered, for just a few minutes.

Parmesan Crisps

8 tablespoons finely grated Parmesan (Parmigiano Reggiano is best)

YOU WILL NEED
1 sheet of 'Bakewell' or parchment paper
Baking tray

Draw out eight circles with a 12.5cm (5in) diameter, or eight rectangles measuring 12.5cm (5in) x 4cm (1½in), on the sheet of paper. Place the paper on a baking tray.

Preheat the oven to 180°C/350°F/gas mark 4.

Carefully fill the marked-out shapes with grated Parmesan. Spread the cheese in an even layer to the edges of the circles or rectangles. Cook in the preheated oven for 15–20 minutes until golden and bubbling. Remove from the oven and allow to cool on the tray.

Parmesan Crisps can be moulded into shapes just before they become cold: use a rolling pin as a mould. These are best eaten fresh, but they can be stored in an airtight box.

Sweet Geranium Jelly

We have a collection of sweetly scented geraniums growing on the dining-room window sills: each plant has its own perfume and flavour. Of all the different varieties, Pelargonium graveolens is the one we use most in the kitchen, and its haunting flavour is particularly success-ful in this jelly.

MAKES 3KG (6½LB)

2.7kg (6lb) cooking apples (we use Bramley seedlings or a mixture of these and crab apples)
2.5 litres (4¼ pints) water

6–8 large sweet geranium leaves
(*Pelargonium graveolens*)
2 lemons
Sugar

6–7 geranium leaves

Wash the apples and cut into quarters, but do not remove either the peel or the core. Windfalls may be used but be sure to cut out the bruised parts. Put the apples into a large saucepan with the water, the geranium leaves and the thinly pared rind of the lemons. Cook over a medium heat until the apples have dissolved into a pulp – this takes about 30 minutes. Turn the pulp into a jelly bag and leave to drip until all the juice has come through – usually overnight.

Preheat the oven to 150°C/325°F/gas mark 2.

Measure the juice into a preserving pan and allow 450g (1lb) sugar to each 600ml (1 pint) of juice. Warm the sugar in the low oven. Squeeze the lemons, strain the juice and add it to the preserving pan. Bring to the boil and add the warm sugar. Meanwhile turn up the heat of the oven to 180°C/350°F/gas mark 4.

Stir the mixture in the preserving pan over a high heat until the sugar has dissolved. Then boil rapidly without stirring for about 8–10 minutes. In the meantime, sterilize the jars in the pre-heated hot oven for about 10 minutes.

To test for a set, put a little jelly on to a chilled plate and cool for a minute or two; then press with your finger: if the jelly wrinkles slightly, it will set. Alternatively, use a sugar thermometer to test for setting point. The jelly will set when the thermometer registers 104°C (220°F).

Skim the jelly, put a geranium leaf into the sterilized pots and fill each one with hot jelly. Cover and seal immediately. Label and store in a cool dry place.

Variations on Geranium Jelly

Clove Jelly

Add 3–6 cloves to the apples as they stew and put a clove in each pot. Serve on bread or scones.

Mint Jelly

Add 4–6 large sprigs of fresh mint to the apples while they are stewing and add 3–4 tablespoons of finely chopped fresh mint to the jelly just before it is potted. Serve with lamb.

Rosemary Jelly

Add two sprigs of rosemary to the apples as they stew and put a tiny sprig into each pot. Serve with lamb.

Candied Julienne of Lemon Peel

This candied peel can be stored in an airtight container for many weeks. Use it for decorating cakes and the Lemon Ice-cream on page 44.

2 lemons
Stock syrup made with 170g (6oz) sugar and 175ml (6fl oz) water, cooked together for 2 minutes

Peel the lemons very thinly with a swivel-top peeler (be careful not to include the white pith). Cut the strips into fine
julienne. Put in a saucepan with 2 cups of cold water and simmer for 5 minutes. Remove from the pan, refresh in cold water and repeat the process again. Put the juliennes in a saucepan with the syrup and cook gently until the lemon looks translucent. Remove with a slotted spoon and allow to cool on on a wire rack or on baking parchment. When cold sprinkle with caster sugar.

Chocolate Caraque

115g (4oz) dark chocolate

Melt the chocolate and spread it thinly with a palette knife onto a marble slab. Allow it to set almost completely and then, using a sharp knife or clean paint scraper, shave off long, thin scrolls. Use a slight sawing action and keep your hand upright. This is fun to do but there's quite a lot of skill involved. You'll get good at it with practice, and you can always eat the rejects!

Above: Sweet Geranium Jelly. Of all the different varieties of geranium we have at Ballymaloe Cookery School, *Pelargonium graveolens* is the one we use most in the kitchen. Its haunting flavour is particularly successful in this jelly.

Index

191

First published in paperback in 2007 by
Kyle Cathie Limited
122 Arlington Road
London, NW1 7HP
www.kylecathie.com

First hardback was published in 1997

ISBN 978 1 85626 709 0

Text © 1997 Darina Allen
Food photography © 1997 Michelle Garrett
Photography © 1997 Melanie Eclare
Designed by Paul Welti
Typesetting by Peter Howard
Home economy by Fionnuala Ryan and Jane Suthering

Darina Allen is hereby identified as the author of this work in accordance with Section 77 of the Copyright, Designs and Patents Act 1988

A CIP catalogue record for this title is available from the British Library

Printed and bound in Singapore by Tien Wah Press

Photographic acknowledgements

A–Z Botanical Collection: Martin Stankewitz, 20.
Timmy Allen: 2–3; 15; 16 top; 17; 56 bottom.
Kevin Dunne: 102. Melanie Eclare: 1; 4–5; 7–14; 16 bottom; 18 all photos; 19; 24–5; 28 side bar; 29; 30 side bar; 32–3 background; 34; 36 side bar; 50–5; 56 top right; 57; 58 bottom; 72–3; 76 side bar; 78 side bar; 80 bottom; 82; 84–5; 90 side bar; 91; 96–101; 103; 110 bottom; 126; 140–7; 156 side bar; 158 side bar; 166 side bar; 168 side bar.
The Garden Picture Library: Philippe Bonduel, 22.
Michelle Garrett: 20–3; 26 side bar; 28; 31; 32 inset; 35; 37–49; 58 side bar; 59–71; 74–5; 77; 79; 80 side bar; 82–3; 86–9; 90 bottom; 92–5; 104–9; 110 side bar; 111–125; 129–139; 148–155; 156 top; 157–165; 167; 169–181.